To: Vonita,

His Story, History and His Secret

Life Through the Eyes of 105 Year Old Otis Grandville Clark

DR. GWEN WILLIAMS AND STAR WILLIAMS

author-HOUSE®

AuthorHouse™
1663 Liberty Drive, Suite 200
Bloomington, IN 47403
www.authorhouse.com
Phone: 1-800-839-8640

First published by AuthorHouse 2/4/2008

ISBN: 978-1-4343-6820-1 (sc)

Printed in the United States of America
Bloomington, Indiana

This book is printed on acid-free paper.

Front Photo Credit: Star Williams (Otis G. Clark)
Back Photo Credit: Gary D. Avey (Ford Model T Coupe Sepia)

Table of Contents

Preface

We wrote this book in honor and to celebrate Otis Dad Clark's 105th birthday. He is a man of adventure and went on a cruise for his 105th birthday. He deserves to enjoy life and live it to the fullest. He wants his birthday cruise an annual event so you are invited. Consider this your invitation. For more information, please visit www.LifeEnrichmentInc.com.

The objective is to tell you Dad's story or His Story. His story is a derivative of God's story, which is also His Story meaning God's story and the History that reflects Dad's life and the events around it. The number one question Dad is asked is, "What is your secret to a long life?" So we have His Secret and nuggets throughout the book.

The memoir aggregates of past events; and critical times in Dad's life. The wide range of events occurring is in chronological order leading from the past to the present and even into the future. We have recorded oral history from Dad and narrative description of past events.

Our prayer is that the records and interpretations of past events involving Dad's life is remembered to encourage you to forgive, to love, and to live life to the fullest, and never forget that on God's side which Dad says is the winning side!

We hope you are blessed, inspired, and encouraged by Dad's memoir. Dad is 105 years old and full of life. Everyday we are around him we are amazed at the things he remembers, says, and does. He is a modern day miracle and a sign and wonder. His mind is sharp. He can state facts, dates, streets, and is a prolific reader.

He has had check ups at the doctor and they have reported he has a heart of a thirty five year old man. He is not on any medications and has no illnesses. He is a healthy eater, loves the Lord, still drives, and exercises daily.

He is a man who knows how to forgive because he has been forgiven. He sees the best in every situation and is ready to set new objectives and goals in his life or as he often says he keeps up with the young people. He follows those who have vision. He always stays ready for what ever the day may bring. When it is time to go he dresses himself, takes pride in his looks and is ready to go.

He has been an evangelist since 1927. He lived through the 1921 Tulsa, Oklahoma Race Riot, been shot at, went through the Influenza outbreak and delivered medicines to those who were sick. In addition, he went through the Great Depression, and went to the Chicago Worlds Fair in 1933, Azusa Street Mission and many other historical milestones he has crossed over, visited or went through. Please enjoy as your chronicle through his life, and history.

On God's Side,
Dr. Gwen Williams and Star Williams

Chapter 1

– Happy 105th Birthday Dad! –

Keep the Faith: Dad Strong at 105

If there was a Scripture that would describe Dad, it would be 1 Timothy 4:7. The paraphrased version reads, "He is fighting the good fight, finishing the race, and keeping the faith." Dad sees his life as being on the winning side. He is known to preach the infamous message, "If you are on God's side you are a winner; and if you are not on God's side, you are a loser." When you think you can't win or won't make it, see the finish line—don't quit now, you're almost there.

Dad is known as the one who lives by Dale Carnegies' saying, "Most of the things in the world have been accomplished by people who have kept on trying when there seemed to be no hope."[1] He is one who never says "can't." His secret is doing all things through Christ who strengthens him (Philippians 4:13) and relying totally on the Word of God. He turns every day of the year into a positive opportunity in his life. He is a tough person who has lasted through tough times.

He believes you should learn to never give up or say you can't—but with Christ's help, you can do all things. We can push past the difficult times, receive inner healing, life, health, energy and power to make the impossible possible.

Dad was born in Indian Territory, delivered medicine to people's home during the influenza epidemic, survived the 1921 Tulsa Race Riot, was jailed for selling alcohol during Prohibition, went through the Great Depression, outlived four wives, and survived many other situations and circumstances in life. Dad has overlooked the pain and heartache in his life by walking through life with forgiveness.

Many people say they will never live to be 100 years old. Some have even said "Give me 68 good years, and I will be happy." Dad has an optimistic outlook on life and living. As an heir, he believes in the impossible. He has achieved so many things in his life that it has seemed impossible. He has triumphed and overcome so many obstacles.

Dad is meek, kind, and gentle, but let him get something in his mind that he wants to accomplish and he becomes determined. When he was 97, he decided one day that he needed to take care of some business in Seattle, Washington where he used to live. He left Atlanta, Georgia, driving in his car, went from there to Seattle. He made it there and back driving by himself! Yes, he is a man with a great adversity quotient.

When we say we can, we become tough-minded people who have a strong faith.[2] When times are difficult, dark, dreary, and gloomy, we must find hope and perceive success in these difficult times. When we learn to prioritize our possibilities, all the options we have, and the prospective that can give us freedom, we can meet our goals and live an abundant life. Let us prioritize our chance of having a healthy life by staying on God's side, which is the winning side.

Even if you do experience some defeat, we must remember there is always a comeback. You can beat the odds that most people estimate regarding life. No matter how many times you may have been defeated by the unhealthy, ungodly act in your life, you can repent and stay on God's side. You will beat the odds and overcome the temptations. No matter how hard it may seem, you will walk in victory.

Through life's experiences and walking with God, you can be assured of success with God and you will have help to keep you and get you on course. Once you begin to move in the right way you will be inspired to turn every negative into a positive and to make every day the best day of your life. Make the turn to tough-minded faith and make the hurdle to fantastic, successful living.[3] Your life will never be the same.

Dad is *always* optimistic. When you are around him, it becomes contagious. Everywhere he goes he has a positive affect on the people he meets. People always want to know his secret to longevity. Everyone wants to know—young and old alike. They ask what he eats, what type of lifestyle he lives, or they ask something about his health. Additionally, people want to know his thoughts and feelings.

When Dad was 90 he was at a church speaking, prior to getting up, the children behind him were restless, talking and not paying attention. One of the boys, said, "Shh, shh—hey everyone, be quiet, I want to hear what this 90 year old man has to say." He got his other peers to listen. Dad with his strong voice told them about Jesus, the story of the prodigal son, and about being on the winning side. In 2008 at 105 years old, can you imagine how many people are listening to Dad *now*? In his lifetime, he has spoken to many people of many walks of life. It has been estimated that since 2000 he has done 84 radio, television, or newspaper interviews.

He believes in looking nice all the time. He wears a suit and tie everyday. Some days, he has on a three piece suit. He always wears a hat—his bishop's hat, Dobbs, Stetson, a brim, or a Derby. The only shoe he wears is a Stacey Adam. He has them in many different colors.

Once at a fancy banquet while Dad was sitting at the head table he used his linen dinner napkin to shine his rings. Well, the program had not started yet, but the room was full. Later he decided to shine his Stacey Adams shoes with the dinner napkin. Mind you, the shoes were already shining. At 105 he still loves to look nice every day. He looks good, and I am sure that plays a part of how he feels. People always notice him and are also affected by his appearance. You know the old sayings appearance is important to how we feel, and you never get a second chance to make a first impression.

He leaves a great impression on the people he meets and the quality of life he leads. Is it any wonder that people want to be around Dad, a healthy positive 105 year old? He does not have time to focus on negative thoughts, words and attitudes about himself or others. He says it will not help us determine a healthy cause; they only bring up negative and unhappy moods and actions that lead to destructive tendencies and mindsets. When the mind focuses on the negative, poisons are released into the blood, which cause more unhappiness and negativity. This is the way to fail in your health. He does not have high blood pressure, anxiety or stress. As Dad would say, stop all the fuss; get rid of frustration and disappointment.

Stop and Smell the Roses

Dad is one who literally enjoys the daily journey of life. It does not matter if we are on an airplane, in a car, walking or sitting around; he enjoys the scenery, narrates, loves the people, and stops to smell the roses. In retrospect, each of our lives is a self-fulfilling prophecy. We have to determine the cause by deciding not to remain the same. So many times it is easy to continue to keep the hurt and pain that can be instrumental in causing us to miss out on abundant life. We can settle on and conclude that we have to remain the way we are for the rest of our lives. It is when we establish, and agree with ourselves that we stop and smell the roses and let go of the pain of rejection, hurt, and uncertainty. When these issues are resolved we can determine the end result.

The reason the things we do will bring us to the point of why we have to push past the pain and hurt of our past is because it grounds us to the origin of the problem whether or not it is due to emotional and medical issues or diet. Knowing the source and foundation will help us become overcomers. Dad wants us to reach a point where you are willing to make a change and progressively change your mental attitude that admits into the mind thoughts, words and images that are conducive to your spiritual growth, development and success. It is a mental concept that expects good and positive results. Dad determines the cause to be optimistic. His mind expects happiness, joyfulness, health and a positive outcome everyday. What the mind perceives it conceives. How many people 105 years old do you know first of all, but how many do you know who have a sharp mind, fully aware of what is going on, has a good memory and the joy of the Lord?

Dad thinks we have to think like heirs of Christ, but many of us do not because we have not accepted the point that we are heirs. Some may consider changing their ways as just nonsense, and others make fun of people who believe and accept it. Among the people who expect to walk in the promises and His fullness are those who are effective and get the results. Dad is always positive about accomplishing his goals. If he is driving cross country or doing a small task he is quite positive in thinking that he can reach his goals. How many people in their nineties or hundreds would seriously think about driving cross the country? So many times we get set in our old way of doing things. The older we get, the more set we become. Dad is always open to try new things. Changing old patterns of thinking and bad habits can bring about new perspectives that are optimistic, useful and effective. How many people do you know, who stop to think about what the power of being optimistic can do?

Health

Dad does not have any medical issues, his check ups and the studies that have been done on him show him to be very healthy. His actions over the years, along with living a healthy life are the rewards he is experiencing today. What he eats does play a vital role in his health. He has self-control. How many times are we disobedient to our doctors, self, or family when we know that certain foods are harmful to our health? We have to change our eating habits and eliminate unhealthy foods which can hinder us in the long run. Dad has a simple plan. He knows when he has had enough. He eats in moderation, eats healthy and stays active.

Dad's wants us to walk in a life of action. When we realize that we have to take action we can situate ourselves to receive what is best for us. If we do not take action we will remain and exist in the same stupor. Insanity is doing the same thing expecting different results. So make a change. Become active. Choose to live an exciting life.

When we take a stand, we walk in our convictions, certainty, and the assurances that are promised with living a healthy lifestyle. Our passions and fervor will be expressed by a belief system, principles and faith that we perpetuate through life's convictions. Let us stand up for our convictions.

The powerful goal of being an heir is to receive and provide excellent service. When we do what is functional and practical then we can enhance our lifestyle and contribute directly to our health. In order to turn the mind toward the positive, inner healing and intentional action and exercise are required. Attitude and thoughts do not change overnight.

Dad always sees the best in every situation. When he looks at things he visualizes only favorable and beneficial situations. He uses encouraging words in his mind and positive self talk. Dad always smiles. He thinks more often about delightful things. Disregard any feelings of laziness or a desire to quit.

Dad is always ready to go. If you ask is he tired, he always says, "Tired of what?" Dad says if you persist, you can change the way your mind thinks and you will reach your goals. Once a negative thought enters your mind, you have to be aware of it and try to replace it with a constructive one and stand on the promises of God. The negative thought will try again to enter your mind, and then you have to replace it again with a positive one. We are urged in Philippians 4:8—"Whatever is true, whatever is noble, whatever is right, whatever is pure, whatever is lovely, whatever is admirable— if anything is excellent or praiseworthy—think about such things." Persistence is another secret of Dad's.

He is proactive in his walk with God on a daily basis. He avoids the temptation that comes his way and the conditions that make him feel internal struggles and make him not want to act. You will never make it to 105 without God's help and changing the pessimistic action with optimistic action and focus on His Word. Do not throw in the towel, but keep taking the actions that are beneficial, excellent, and cheerful in your mind. As Dad often says, fight the good fight of faith, keep the faith, and if Satan is bothering you, tell him to get behind you.

When you change your actions, you have to realize the importance of repetitious affirmations. This process will help you reach your goals, take the right actions, and see yourself in a new light, healthy, whole, physically capable, and serving Christ to the fullest.

Chapter 2

– The Clark's and Slavery –

The history of slavery in the United States was between 1619-1865, and it began shortly after the English settlers came to Virginia and continued until the promulgation of the 13th Amendment to the U.S. Constitution.[4] In the beginning of slavery there was what was termed as indentured servitude, but this concept only lasted up to seven years for whites and blacks. In 1662 the American incarnation of slavery was promulgated by a court ruling. [5]During the later part of the 17th century, slavery was more common in the Southern colonies than in the North.

From the 1640s to 1865, people of African descent were lawfully enslaved within the confines of the United States, mostly by whites, but also by some American Indians and free blacks.

The 1860 United States census specifies fewer than 385,000[6] individuals (e.g. 1.4% of white Americans in the country and 4.8% of southern whites) owned one or more slaves.[7] Before the Civil War, one out of every four families had slaves in the South. Ninety-five percent of blacks lived in the South, comprising one-third of the population there as opposed to 1% of the population of the North. [8]

Approximately 12 million black Africans were shipped to the Americas from the 17th to the 19th centuries. Of these, 5.4% (645,000) were brought to what is now the United States. [9]The slave population in the United States had grown to four million by the 1860 Census.

Dad's grandfather, Aaron Clark, grew up as a slave's son. He lived on a plantation. The plantation was in Austin, Texas in a little town that later became known as Clarksville. Those who lived there had to have sources of supply to meet the needs of daily living. Many plantation workers grew cotton, vegetables, and made clothes from the cotton. Dad's grandfather's trade was brick making; some people made their own furniture, were blacksmiths, or were carpenters. These slaves knew the trade and were respected by other slaves and the master.

During this time in history, women slaves helped deliver babies and raise children. These women are called midwives. They delivered babies for both masters and slaves. Dad's grandmother was a cook. Many of the women slaves were master expert cooks, sewed, and quilted for slaves and masters.

Dad's grandparents grew up in an era near the end of slavery. Two types of slaves existed—field slaves or house slaves. Dad said the cooks had better lives than the field slaves. The house slaves worked in the master's house. The master was referred to as "Mr. Charlie" or "Mr. Joe"—"Mr. was the main thing." The wife was called a mistress, and she did not do much cooking. Sometimes the house slaves lived in what was called the "big house." The women were called "mammies." Many times the mammies breast fed and were close to the master's children.

Often times, house slaves were dressed in nice clothes because the lady boss picked their clothing. Many of the men wore white shirts with bow ties and served the guests and the family. Many of the house slaves lived in nicer shanties. Dad thought the house slaves had it better than the field slaves.

Many times the master's family looked at the house slaves as part of their family; they were never treated equally, but they had some favor. As quiet as it was kept, some of the house slaves were related to the family because some of the masters had children with the mammies.

The house slaves went off the plantation to help with special occasions and events. In most of the South, it was illegal to teach a black to read or write. The slaves that could read had been taught by the master's children. The mammies' responsibility was helping with the needs of the house and the master's children.

Many slaves did not want to live in slavery. Dad's Grandpa Clark wanted to be free as well. Slaves found it hard, and many wanted to be free and leave the plantation. They had no money or clothes. If they ran, they could have been sold, killed, hung, burned, or whipped. Even after slavery ended, Grandpa Clark had to be careful when he left to come to Oklahoma, which was Indian Territory. If you lived in Indian Territory, you were considered to have some freedom.

Sometimes slaves who were trying to escape would walk to their destinations. Many would travel at night, crossing rivers, canals, creeks, and going through woods. Even after slavery, patrols would catch former slaves and get rewards for returning them. If the slave was caught running away, he or she would be punished. Many people did not obey the law freeing the slaves and did not want to accept the transition.[10]

Life on the plantations was difficult, and no thought was given to the cultural traditions of blacks. [11]In the slave market, people were treated as equal to animals and separated from their wives; and frequently children were taken from their mothers. Under the plantation system, gang labor was the way of employment.[12] Masters were often cruel, unsympathetic, and very strict about working. Retribution was at the judgment of the master.

Family and African links were severed. Housing, food, and clothing were of poor quality for most slaves.[13] Rape of a female slave was not considered unlawful. If someone trespassed on the master's property, it was considered unlawful, but slaves could not present evidence in court against whites.

African-American's were very instrumental in the wealth of the U.S. in the first half of the 19th century.[14] Slave labor helped build American fruit with African roots. The enormous cotton industry began to fall because slave labor ended. The North had its victory in the Civil War, and the South lost its cotton revenue. [15]The industries began to prosper and helped in the industrial economy in the United States.

History of Slavery in America[16]

1619   The first African slaves arrive in Virginia.

1787   Slavery is made illegal in the Northwest Territory. The US Constitution states that Congress may not ban the slave trade until 1808.

1793   Eli Whitney's invention of the cotton gin greatly increases the demand for slave labor.

1793   A federal fugitive slave law is enacted, providing for the return slaves who had escaped and crossed state lines.

1800   Gabriel Prosser, an enslaved African-American blacksmith, organizes a slave revolt intending to march on Richmond, Virginia. The conspiracy is uncovered, and Prosser and a number of the rebels are hanged. Virginia's slave laws are consequently tightened.

1808   Congress bans the importation of slaves from Africa.

1820   The Missouri Compromise bans slavery north of the southern boundary of Missouri.

1822   Denmark Vesey, an enslaved African-American carpenter who had purchased his freedom, plans a slave revolt with the intent to lay siege on Charleston, South Carolina. The plot is discovered, and Vesey and 34 coconspirators are hanged.

1831   Nat Turner, an enslaved African-American preacher, leads the most significant slave uprising in American history. He and his band of followers launch a short, bloody rebellion in Southampton County, Virginia. The militia quells the rebellion, and Turner is eventually hanged. As a consequence, Virginia institutes much stricter slave laws.

1831 William Lloyd Garrison begins publishing the Liberator, a weekly paper that advocates the complete abolition of slavery. He becomes one of the most famous figures in the Abolitionist Movement.

1846 The Wilmot Proviso, introduced by Democratic representative David Wilmot of Pennsylvania, attempts to ban slavery in territory gained in the Mexican War. The proviso is blocked by Southerners but continues to enflame the debate over slavery.

1849 Harriet Tubman escapes from slavery and becomes one of the most effective and celebrated leaders of the Underground Railroad.

1850 The continuing debate if territory gained in the Mexican War should be open to slavery is decided in the Compromise of 1850: California is admitted as a free state, Utah and New Mexico territories are left to be decided by popular sovereignty, and the slave trade in Washington, DC is prohibited. It also establishes a much stricter fugitive slave law than the original, passed in 1793.

1852 Harriet Beecher Stowe's novel, Uncle Tom's Cabin is published. It becomes one of the most influential works to stir anti-slavery sentiments.

1854 Congress passes the Kansas-Nebraska Act, establishing the territories of Kansas and Nebraska. The legislation repeals the Missouri Compromise of 1820 and renews tensions between anti- and pro-slavery factions.

1857 The Dred Scott case holds that Congress does not have the right to ban slavery in states, and slaves are not citizens.

1859 John Brown and 21 followers capture the federal arsenal at Harpers Ferry, Virginia (which is now West Virginia), in an attempt to launch a slave revolt.

1861 The Confederacy is founded when the Deep South secedes and the Civil War begins.

1863 President Lincoln issues the Emancipation Proclamation, declaring "that all persons held as slaves" within the Confederate state "are, and henceforward shall be free."

1865 The Civil War ends. Lincoln is assassinated. The Thirteenth Amendment abolishes slavery throughout the United States. On June 19, slavery in the United States effectively ended when 250,000 slaves in Texas finally received the news that the Civil War had ended two months earlier.[17]

Chapter 3

– Clarksville, Texas –

Texas was formally admitted to the Union as a slave state in 1846. The census in 1847 was the first official one that was taken. It was reported that Texas' population counted 38,753 slaves and 102,961 whites.[18] In East Texas there were enslaved person runaways in lower Colorado and Brazos rivers. Because of the exodus of slaves running away a law was passed in 1848.[19]

The state legislature aimed at punishing those who might help escaping slaves. Anyone helping slaves plan a rebellion would be punished with death. Ship captains assisting runaways would receive from two to ten years in the penitentiary. Anyone who would steal or entice away a slave from his or her owner would receive three to fifteen years of hard labor.

Free persons of color who aided a slave in escaping would receive from three to five years in the penitentiary.[20]

Dad's grandpa was from Clarksville, originally a Black community half a mile outside of the city limits of Austin, Texas. Clarksville remains a melting pot of art and culture to this day. Houses have increased greatly in price due to the location of the neighborhood and all it has to offer. [21]West Lynn Café, a popular vegetarian restaurant, is there, as well as Jeffrey's for fine dining. Tourists may also enjoy a visit to Nau Enfield Drug, where they sale old-fashioned malts.[22]

Jake Billingsley is a white youth who grew up with black families because his dad was the minister at St. James Episcopal Church in East Austin. Billingsley moved to Clarksville in the 1970s after a black co-worker sold him a house. Living in the same house for years, the home appraised at a magnitude more than the original cost.[23]

Billingsley has been a community organizer. He recalls the history: "[Clarksville] was founded by Charles Clark a freedman in approximately 1870. Governor Elisha M. Pease of Texas had deeded land to some of his former slaves.[24] Slaves could not own any property unless sanctioned by a slave master or someone in position to do so."[25] According to Dad, Aaron Clark, his grandfather, and Henry Clark, his father, were descendants of families from Clarksville. Dad states that his father and grandfather owned property and some of the plantation land that formed that first settlement of Clarksville.

According to Dr. Charles Urdy, this community thrived so much and was known as this "freedom town." In the 1970s it became recognized by the National Register, which registers national historic places[26] and sites in the United States as one of only two truly black national historic districts in the entire United States.[27] (The other one is Martin Luther King's birthplace in Atlanta, Georgia.)[28]

Urdy also states, "Pauline Brown moved to Clarksville at an early age." The community centered at that time, on the Sweet Home Baptist Church and family relationships. [29] They had to get many services, like schools, miles away in east Austin. Brown recalled that the comfortable life in Clarksville suddenly gave way when the MoPac Expressway came to life off the drafting table.[30] Urdy said, "Clarksville started seeing a change when the city council decided to build an expressway on the west side of town. That included coming across the whole area of Clarksville." [31] MoPac's construction eviscerated the heart of Clarksville. The remaining families, those whose properties weren't in the path, eventually found development knocking on their doors and sold out long ago. Brown is probably the oldest original resident of the neighborhood.[32] The cost to live there is quite expensive now. Since the mid-1950s, Brown has soldiered on, striving to protect as much of the old neighborhood and its history as she can. Many changes have taken place in Clarksville over the years.[33]

Dad's grandfather, while living in Clarksville, had cattle and was a brick maker. The bricks were used for the streets. His grandmother's name was Ellen Clark, and his grandfather's name was Aaron Clark, but he called them grandma and grandpa. They both left Clarksville in the late 1800's with their four sons and one daughter—Dan, Henry, Aaron Jr., Benny, and Vinnie. They all moved to what was then Indian Territory and now Tulsa, Oklahoma.

During Pease's term, most of the tribes that had once lived in East Texas had been induced to live on reservations. By 1859 these people had been deported to Indian Territory (now Oklahoma). However, raids continued on the western frontier for another 15 years. The Comanche, Cheyenne, and Kiowa held out the longest, not surrendering until 1875.[34]

Dad's mother, Effie Moore, and father, Henry Clark, married possibly in Chandler, Oklahoma, which was also Indian Territory. Dad was born in 1903 in Meridian, Indian Territory. Oklahoma received its statehood when Dad was four. Meridian is 43 miles north-east of Oklahoma City and 7.5 miles from Langston, Oklahoma.

Chapter 4

– Oklahoma Promise of Black Paradise –

Grandpa Clark heard about the good things going on in Indian Territory, which is now Oklahoma. Many others heard, too. The history of African-Americans in Oklahoma is very different from other places in the United States. Many African-Americans originally came to Indian Territory on the "Trail of Tears," as Indian slaves. Now Grandpa Clark, when he came, he was a settler. Blacks who came were cowboys, settlers, farmers, or gunfighters.

In 1907, Oklahoma received its statehood. African-Americans greatly populated the region. There were more blacks than Indians and first- and second-generation Europeans. Oklahoma became known for all the black settlements. [35]There were more black towns in Oklahoma than in the entire rest of the United States. Oklahoma was known for it civil rights stances, and production of great music—especially jazz. Twenty-seven black settlements grew to encompass 10% of Indian Territory's population. [36]

On July 17, 1863 in what is known today as Muskogee, Oklahoma, just on the outskirt, black soldiers fought in the Civil War and were first to fight with whites during what is known as the Battle of Honey Springs. The blacks broke the confederate center and helped the Union win and take the Arkansas River and the Texas Road.[37] These routes were used for major transport. This in turn gave the Union place in Indian Territory, and it is a place they have never given up.

Black soldiers built Oklahoma forts, fought bandits, cattle thieves, Mexican revolutionaries (including Pancho Villa), and policed borders during the land runs.[38] They also played a critical role in the Indian Wars of the late 1800s, earning the respect of Native Americans who gave them the name "Buffalo Soldiers." [39]

In 1866, one year after the Civil War ended, Congress passed a bill providing resources for black troops—what became the 9th and 10th Cavalry. The 10th Calvary was stationed at Fort Gibson and the 9th was stationed at Fort Sill.

African-American settlers in Oklahoma could vote, study, and move about with relative freedom shortly after the Civil War. Brochures were handed out to people in the South urging blacks to join land runs in Indian Territory. People were told to come and build their black businesses and cities with the goal and hope of becoming the first predominately Black state.

Pamphlets promising a black paradise in Oklahoma lured tens of thousands of former slaves from the South. Today, many of Oklahoma's original black settlements and districts are gone, but those that remain still host rodeos, Juneteenth celebrations, and community reunions.

Indian Territory

Dad's grandparents on his mother's side were Grandma and Papa Hodge. He does not know their first names. Grandpa Hodge was his step-grandfather. They live in Meridian, Oklahoma. Dad was given the name of "Otis Grandville" by a neighbor and friend of his grandparents. Dad grew up with his mother's brother's children. Their names were Uncle Socks, Tom, Adair, and Mantillas. Dad, as a young fellow, admired and looked up to them.

The Hodges were considered sharecroppers. Sharecropping is a system of agriculture or agricultural production where a landowner allows a sharecropper to use the land in return for a share of the crop produced on the land. Sharecropping has a long history, and there are a wide range of different situations and types of agreements. Some are governed by tradition, others by law, and others through slavery.

On the Hodge's farm, they picked cotton. Their background was similar to Grandparent Clark's. They had cows, horses, and mules. Dad was once bitten by a mule. The uncles would swim in the pond and threw him in the pond, and he had no choice but to learn to swim. These were fun and exciting years for him.

He was raised in Meridian until his mother Effie got a job working in Tulsa. Dad's father was not around. During this time, Henry Clark was a porter on the train and his mother and father had separated.

Meridian was one of the main stops for the Frisco Train. So Dad and his mother left Meridian and went to Tulsa on the train. His siblings, Almeda and Bernard, were already in Tulsa at his grandparent Clark's home.

Dad's first memories of his childhood in Tulsa were of being raised in Grandma Ellen's and Grandpa Aaron Clark's home. Grandpa Clark had a hacks and one horse to pull it. He would haul things for whites who lived in south Tulsa. He also continued his brick making in Chandler, Oklahoma. Grandma Clark stayed home and worked around the house and took care of him, Almeda, and Bernard.

Grandpa Aaron looked liked an Indian and was good friends with the Mohawk and Creek Indians. His grandfather's home had an outhouse, and they drank water from the well.

Another memory at the Clark's home was when Dr. Bridgewater came to the house when he fell; the doctor put snuff down in the wound and the hand became badly infected. It took three months for it to completely heal, and he was in severe pain.

Dad started school at Hartford School which was one block east of Greenwood. He learned the alphabet, geography, English, and reading, writing and Arithmetic. He remembers being in the fifth or sixth grade. He was around ten or eleven years old. He went on to Booker T. Washington High School. This opened in 1913. He enthusiastically states that "I was the first class to go to the new school."

One of Dad's good friends was named Cliff; he lived on Hartford Street, and Dad lived on Archer. They loved to play baseball, go skating, and make go-carts so they could race down the steep hill on Detroit. They loved to fish and swim in the Arkansas River too. He had other friends name Julius and his brother Elmer. They would swim in the country water pond way out on North Pine almost everyday in the summer.

They all played hooky from school but soon found out it did not pay. He remembers being arrested on one of those days by the black chief of police, Barnie Clever. Dad and his friend Cliff stole a bike from the south side of Tulsa. Clever came to arrest Dad at Grandpa Clark's home. Mr. Clever told him, "Come go with me!" He was arrested and the bike was returned. That day they were playing hooky from school so Clever took him to the Hartford School, and he went back to class. Cleaver's home is still in Tulsa on Greenwood and preserved as an historical site.

Chapter 5

– Dad's Teen Days –

Worldwide Influenza Epidemic

When he was about 14 or 15 years old he got a job. He worked for Dr. Shackles, the owner of Shackles Drug Store on the ten hundred block of South Main. Dad rode on his bike carrying medicine to people who were sick and during that time he also was there when the Influenza epidemic struck America and the world. He delivered the medicine to whites in South Tulsa.

The U.S. Bureau of the Census reported an influenza pandemic of 1918-1919. The first quantitative measurements of the epidemic impact were based on mortality. The report stated, "In the March 4, 1919, issue of the "Weekly Health Index," the death rates for 31 large cities for the period of September 18, 1918-March 1, 1919 were compared to the death rates for the same period in 1917-1918, and the difference between them was calculated as the "excess mortality" during the epidemic."[40] In the fall months of October and November there were 300,000 American causalities. The total that died was over a half million Americans in a ten month period. The total in the world was more than 50,000,000 people.[41]

During the time of the epidemic in Oklahoma there were little or no records available for families who were very poor. Also, the poor could not afford the grave stones and people were dying so fast there were many graves that were not marked. There were some newspapers that listed names for people who died at the start of the epidemic, but as the numbers increased they would only list the number of people in the community who died since the last newspaper was published. The same was true with the doctors who were over worked; they stopped issuing death certificates and just kept records of the numbers of deaths. The deaths certificates issued at that time were by a doctor who had time to file one.

It was also reported that some of the families who were ancestral families did not have death certificates filed due to the mass epidemic, as well. Some local newspapers listed obituaries of the more prominent residents of their community or if the death occurred by unusual circumstances.[42]

Dad's Mother

Dad's mother worked in downtown Tulsa on 1st street off of Main at one of the leading hotels. She was one of the maids. She and Henry divorced when Dad was a young boy and Henry remarried in Kansas City, Missouri to Lena. Effie married a man named Walker. Dad left his Grandparent Clark's home and moved with his mother. Walker was a whiskey maker. Effie had a baby by Walker, and Clark's new sister's name was Gladys Walker. Walker took care of Dad for a few years. Walker and Effie later had irreconcilable differences. Effie later married Tom Bryant. Dad and his family left and moved in with his step father, Bryant. He was a builder and in the union.

Dad Moves to Kansas City, Missouri

While living with Walker, Dad's biological father Henry came to Tulsa; and for the first time, at the age of 13 or 14, Dad spent time with his father. Henry Clark took him in his big shiny car to Kansas City, Missouri to start a new life together with Dad and wife Lena.

Dad went to Kansas City and worked in one of the finest hotels on the 3100 Block of Troost Street, near Poseo Street in Kansas City. He was a telephone operator and was handy around the hotel and did other things when he was needed. His father was the concierge. Dad started school in Missouri. He went to a school called Dunbar. During this time, Ella V. Robinson was the principal.

Dad's recreational activities included trips to the zoo and park. He also rode the street car. He lived in the hotel with

Lena, his step mother, and his father. Dad went to Dunbar for about a year. He left and went back to Tulsa.

Dad's Uncle Buck was a major influence in his life. He made corn whiskey, and they lived out in the edition near his cousin Bertha. The whiskey was sold on Greenwood, and Dad helped with deliveries. He stayed in Tulsa and branched off on his own and sold whiskey. To make the corn whiskey Dad would buy corn, yeast, chock, and malt at the feed store. Dad would cook his whiskey down on the river south of Jenks, Oklahoma. Once the whiskey was made they would put it in big five gallon jars that usually held water. The jars would be put in the river to cool them down. Dad would put the jars in his car and head to Greenwood. The jars were sold to individuals on the street. Dad lived in a hotel on Greenwood and Archer.

Filled with discontentment with his delinquent lifestyle, Dad decided he wanted to go back to Kansas and give up the whiskey business. This time he went on his own. His father Henry was still working as a caretaker or porter in the hotel. Dad got a job, this time working in the kitchen as a cook. He cooked flap jacks or pancakes. Dad became a ladies man and had plenty of girlfriends before he got on God's side. With all the running around and wild living, he lost his job and moved back to Tulsa. He stayed with his step father Tom Bryant and his mother.

Chapter 6

– 1921 Tulsa Race Riot –

In May of 1921, when Dad was eighteen years old, the riot broke out and many people were killed. On the day of the riot, Dad was visiting with Jackson on Archer and Greenwood. They were a few blocks from downtown and close to the dividing lines of Blacks and Whites. Jackson was just starting out in the funeral business. Dad and Jackson were acquaintances because Almeda, Dad's sister, had two boys by Jackson.

1921 Tulsa Race Riot [43]

Dad heard gun shots. Men were on the south side of the tracks up in an old mill about three or four stories high. The white men were shooting at black men who were on the street. The black men were trying to protect themselves. They had guns but no rounds to fire. Dad and Jackson's driver were trying to get the ambulance out of the garage to pick up the people who were downtown. The driver was shot in the hand as Dad stood behind him. The injured driver had blood all over his hand, and he dropped his keys and ran back into the funeral home with Jackson. Then Dad left and ran north down the alley on the back of Greenwood almost to Pine Street. He ran until he was at his aunt and cousin's house.

Lady lost everything: 1921 Tulsa Race Riot [44]

Burning down Greenwood [45]

When Dad got there they were frightened and trying to leave Tulsa. They were getting ready to leave in their car. With mayhem all around, Dad got in the back seat of the car with his Aunt Vinnie and Uncle Buck. Aunt Vinnie's daughter, Bertha, was in the front set of the car, and her husband was driving. They were on their way to Claremore to escape from getting killed. On the way to Claremore, after crossing the bridge east of Greenwood about five men with guns stopped the car. They told everyone to get out car. The men took Uncle Buck and Bertha's husband's guns and let them continue to Claremore. Dad recalls, "When we got to Claremore, we went to a colored hotel for one night."

Captured Negros on their way to the Convention Hall:
1921 Tulsa Race Riot [46]

*1921 Tulsa Race
Riot* [47]

*Homes burn down:
1921 Tulsa Race
Riot* [48]

Greenwood burned to the ground: 1921 Tulsa Race Riot [49]

Black Wall Street-Greenwood destroyed: 1921 Tulsa Race Riot [50]

Bertha got word
the next day
that the riot had
stopped and the
Salvation Army
and the National
Guard had come to

1921 Tulsa Race Riot[51]

Tulsa to stop the fighting and help the victims. So they all went back to north Tulsa. Aunt Vinnie and Uncle Buck's house was not damaged. Bertha's house was also intact.

Black Wall Street-Greenwood up in smoke: 1921 Tulsa Race Riot[52]

People search in the rubble: 1921 Tulsa Race Riot[53]

The Aftermath: 1921 Tulsa Race Riot[54]

Dad went back and stayed with his cousin Bertha because his mother Effie and Grandmother Clark's home were burned down. His step father, Tom Bryant, was never seen again. The bulldog, Bob, was burned up in the home, too. The Salvation Army built a one room house for Grandma Clark and Effie and Gladys. (Papa Clark had died a few years earlier.) Dad was devastated. He did not understand why anyone would want to kill his step-dad and his dog and burn down his home. He was in shock.

1921 Tulsa Race Riot Picture Gallery[55]

Negro Slain in Tulsa Riot: 1921 Tulsa Race Riot

Transporting bodies from Black Wall Street/Greenwood: 1921 Tulsa Race Riot

Refugees: 1921 Tulsa Race Riot

SATURDAY, JUNE 4, 1921.

The moment that law is destroyed, liberty is lost; and men, left free to enter upon the domains of each other, destroy each other's rights, and invade the field of each other's liberty.—Timothy Titcomb.

IT MUST NOT BE AGAIN

SUCH a district as the old "Niggertown" must never be allowed in Tulsa again. It was a cesspool of iniquity and corruption. It was the cesspool which had been pointed out specifically to the Tulsa police and to Police Commissioner Adkison, and they could see nothing in it. Yet anybody could go down there and buy all the booze they wanted. Anybody could go into the most unspeakable dance halls and base joints of prostitution. All this had been called to the attention of our police department and all the police department could do under the Mayor of this city was to whitewash itself. The Mayor of Tulsa is a perfectly nice, honest man, we do not doubt, but he is guileless. He could have found out himself any time in one night what just one preacher found out.

In this old "Niggertown" were a lot of bad niggers and a bad nigger is about the lowest thing that walks on two feet. Give a bad nigger his booze and his dope and a gun and he thinks he can shoot up the world. And all these four things were to be found in "Niggertown"—booze, dope, bad niggers and guns.

The Tulsa Tribune makes no apology to the Police Commissioner or to the Mayor of this city for having plead with them to clean up the cesspools in this city.

Commissioner Adkison has said that he knew of the growing agitation down in "Niggertown" some time ago and that he and the Chief of Police went down and told the negroes that if anything started they would be responsible.

That is first class conversation but rather weak action. Well, the bad niggers started it. The public would now like to know: why wasn't it prevented? Why were these niggers not made to feel the force of the law and made to respect the law? Why were not the violators of the law in "Niggertown" arrested? Why were they allowed to go on in many ways defying the law? Why? Mr. Adkison; why?

The columns of The Tribune are open to Mr. Adkison for any explanation he may wish to make.

These bad niggers must now be held, and, what is more, the dope selling and booze selling and gun collecting must STOP. The police commissioner, who has not the ability or the willingness to find what a preacher can find and who WON'T stop it when told of it, but merely whitewashes him-

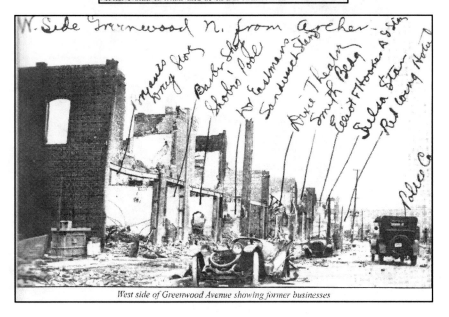

West side of Greenwood Avenue showing former businesses

Wooden shack is temporary home.

Tent with wooden sides as temporary housing.

"Burned beyond recognition."

Tulsa Tribune, Sunday, June 5, 1921

SUNDAY, JUNE 5, 1921.

Aim at excellence and excellence will be attained.
—Bryant.

THE END OF ARGONAUT DAYS

A NEW and better day dawns for Tulsa. Better cities grew out of the ashes of the holocaust that devastated Chicago, San Francisco and Baltimore. Those were disasters that were unforeseen and unavoidable. But as such disasters brought that which is better, so do the disasters that rise like a slowly accumulated cyclone of prejudices and lawlessness, bring in their wake a new conscience and a citizenship that is determined to correct. It is the history of such disasters as that which Tulsa has experienced that that which is bad is made better. By such disasters wrongs are worked into right. To make RIGHT is Tulsa's heroic and righteous resolve today.

Tulsa has a spirit which, however much it may have been dormant, is keenly alive today. It will never again recede to the indifference it has known in the past.

KIWANIS CLUB LAUDS WHITES FOR FIGHTING

Praise for the citizens who beat back the attack of the armed blacks in the downtown district and condemnation for the vandals who wantonly destroyed and pilfered property in the negro district, was contained in a resolution passed by the Kiwanis club today.

The resolution follows:

"Resolved that the Kiwanis club of Tulsa commends the action of those citizens of our city who during the late emergency risked their lives in overcoming, arresting and disarming the negro ruffians who sought by force of arms to intimidate officers and citizens, and impose their will on our fair city; we deplore the loss of the precious lives of innocent persons and of those who fell in attempting to restore order.

"Be It Further Resolved, That we condemn in strongest terms the wanton destruction and pillage of property; we stand in shame at the

Carload of armed whites.

44

The Small Victims of the 1921 Tulsa Race Riot

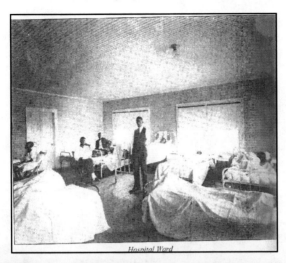

Hospital Ward

Nurse holding infant they called "June Riot."

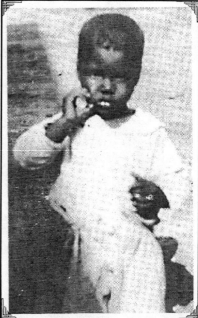

While at his cousin Bertha's home, he helped out with their café. Bertha and her husband made Chock beer and sold dinners. He remembered the people getting drunk and fighting, cussing, and telling tales. Later in life, he learned the Scripture says, "Wine is a mocker and beer is brawler; whoever is led astray by them is not wise" (Proverbs 20:1).

He stayed in Tulsa for a while and worked for Uncle Buck again after things settled. He also resumed whiskey making. He left Bertha's after the Red Cross built a one room house for his mother. Dad lived there for a while. Gladys, Almeda, and Bernard lived with Grandma Clark in her one room shanty. Almeda's two baby boys by Jackson the funeral home owner were Leonard and Robert; they stayed with Grandma Clark too. Five people lived in the one room shanty. Later, Mrs. Elnora, who was Uncle Dan's wife, took Leonard to Pawhuska, Oklahoma to make more room in the house, but Robert stayed with Grandma Clark.

Dad's Grandma Clark got a letter from his dad. He told her he had moved to Milwaukee and left the hotel business. Dad made up in his mind that he would go to Milwaukee to live with his father. He did not want to make the journey alone so he solicited the company of Socks, his mother's brother. Socks said yes and they set off from Tulsa to Milwaukee as hobos to find his father.

Socks and Dad left with only the clothes on their backs. When they got to Chicago, they were hungry. They had to beg and plead for food. A dairy man in the yard gave them breakfast. The man showed him the house, and his cellar that was full of wine. After they had a full belly, they got back on the road to go to Milwaukee. When they arrived in Milwaukee Dad's father, Henry and his wife Lena were gone. They learned that Henry and Lena had moved.

With disappointment, Dad went back to Tulsa and found out his father had written another letter to Grandma Clark and told her he was moving to Los Angeles, California. He left Tulsa in the summer and headed to California. His Uncle Socks did not want to go on another journey, so he settled in Tulsa. Dad got a friend to go with him, so they were hobos all the way to California.

Chapter 7

– Dad Buddies with Stepin Fetchit –

While they were sleeping on the train, one of the railroad officers saw them. They were detained and questioned. They pleaded for the police to let them go. They felt that they had been through enough because of the injustice that happened in Tulsa. They explained their story about the Tulsa riot and received favor from the men.

Dad continued to journey west. He had never seen such beautiful oranges and land as he did between San Bernardino and Los Angeles. They were on the Santa Fe railroad. The long journey proved successful. He made it 70 miles outside of Los Angeles and then finally made it to where his father was staying. When he got there, his father cleaned them up. They had a big dinner at one of the black-owned cafés on the ocean. He ate chicken and steak, and went down to the beach. He had never seen the ocean. He swam in the great Pacific Ocean. He thought he was in paradise.

During this time his father was a houseman for one of the movie stars. Henry got him a job in downtown Los Angeles shining shoes. However, shining shoes was not enough money for Dad; as a result he went back to old habits

Will Rogers and Lincoln Perry/Stepin Fetchit[56]

Stepin Fetchit and Dad

Dad and Stepin Fetchit met in Los Angeles, California in the early 1920's. Stepin met Dad while he was standing outside the Apex Cabaret a few doors down from the Sommersville Hotel. Other entertainers, musicians and show folks were standing around too.

That night Stepin ask Dad to go to a party. Stepin was in his customized Cadillac car. From that day on they were friends. They went to different parties with other famous

Black musicians and entertainers. Stepin would go to Culver City and dance and sing for different shows administered by Whites. Because of segregation Dad would go and wait in the car with his driver while Stepin entertained.

Dad also went to church with him. Stepin would have his driver take him to mass and confessional at the Catholic Church, but Dad would wait for him in the car with his chauffer. Dad went to his home and met his children. During that time Stepin was separated from his wife.

"He was married to Winifred Johnson and had two sons Douglas and Jemajo. Tragically his son Douglas committed suicide on the Pennsylvania turnpike in 1969." [57] During the time Stepin and Dad were friends Dad was bootlegging liquor and went to jail for prohibition and they parted ways. When Dad got out he had accepted Jesus as his Lord and Savior and changed his lifestyle. Later in life Dad went to visit him in the nursing facility and prayed with him.

Stepin Fetchit was the stage name of Lincoln Theodore Monroe Andrew Perry, who claimed a birth-date of May 30, 1902[58] but may have been born as early as 1892.[59]

Perry was born in Key West, Florida. His parents were Indian immigrants. [60] When he was a teenager, Perry became a comedian. He had been educated and could read and was a very clever man. He was a writer for the black newspaper, The Chicago Defender.[61] Then he started acting solely. Perry said his name came from a race horse Step 'n Fetch It. He supposedly won money on the race horse.[62] Some say his name was from a two man show, but he kept the name. Others think the name was given because he was a "Tom." Another claim is that the name was because he had a duo act with another black actor dubbed step and fetch it

Stepin Fetchit is known as the most notorious movie actor in the United States History. He was one of the most gifted comedians ever to do his spiel on the Big Screen. Stepin Fetchit was a millionaire. He was a big star in the 1930s. His acting skills depicted a person who was lazy, who talked a lot of slang, or jive-talked, and was slow-witted. Many Whites looked at Perry's role as a true representation of a Black person.

Perry co-starred with Will Rogers in many films. He was also in John Fords' movie *Steamboat Round the Bend* (1935).[63] Perry's Stepin Fetchit character can be seen as more than holding his own with the great Rogers. In the movies, Rogers is pleased with Stepin Fetchit. Perry's Stepin Fetchit persona could be belittled at any time. When Rogers was satisfied with Perry in the movies, in some ways it helped with the relationships with Blacks and Whites in the United States. But there were still prejudices lurking and a Black person could be belittled at any time for just about anything.

He was also cast with Will Rogers in *County Chairman, David Harum, In Old Kentucky* and *Judge Priest*.[64] Many people thought Perry was the highlight of the movie industry. Irvin Cobb who told Rogers in an interview on the radio on May 19, 1935, he said, "In affection to you, as a tribute to you, I ought to say my favorite performer is Will Rogers, but since I must be honest before this great audience, I'll admit my favorite is Stepin."

Another reporter said, the best person for the part of Cleveland pitcher Satchel Paige, would be Stepin Fetchit, he was the guy who helped to make Will Rogers famous. Watkins wrote that actors including Lionel Barrymore, Will Baxter and Will Rogers, admitted Stepin stole nearly every scene in which he appeared. Once when asked about his relationship with Rogers, Stepin called him America's greatest living humorist.

Rogers related well with the Black entertainer[65]. After all he was taught the rudiments of rope handling by former slaves, who were his first playmates—the children of Rabb and Houston Rogers', former slaves [66]and by Dan Walker, a Black cowboy on his father's ranch. He grew up with a great respect and love for many Black friends and love of their music.

Stepin was the first Black actor to become a millionaire. He did not handle his money correctly. In 1947, Stepin went bankrupt. During the 1940's, times began to change in the movie industry. Blacks began to make their own films and some movies were made specifically for blacks. Unfortunately, in the 1960's he became a charity case.

Stepin Fetchit met many people throughout his career including Buster Keaton, W.C. Fields, Bojangles, Red Skelton and Shirley Temple.[67] Later in life he made friends with the likes of Muhammad Ali, Ben Vereen, Flip Wilson and John Wayne and President Gerald Ford.

Bankrupt after success as a vaudevillian and high paid and popular Black comedian and actor, he landed in a charity hospital in Chicago in 1964. [68]

Stepin Fechit defended his contributions to black entertainment in 1967 in a Newsweek magazine interview saying he "Went in and kicked open doors in Hollywood ... so now Sidney Poitier can come in the front door."

Stepin Fetchit suffered a massive stroke in 1976[69] and lived out life in a temperamental state in the Motion Picture Country Home in California, where he died in 1985.

Stepin Fetchit. Bettmann/CORBIS
© 2006 [70]

He was part of a show where his character was looked at as the "The Laziest Man in the World" as part of a two-man variety show. Many Whites began to watch his show. Many

Blacks say he was the Black movie star who opened doors for others Blacks. [71]

When Stepin auditioned for a role in *In Old Kentucky*,[72] he remained in his disposition as an actor before and after the audition. When some scripts were insulting he would not say them and would act like he was too ignorant.[73]

Perry was condemned and criticized by some of the civil rights leaders. Some of these leaders were against CBS showing Amos and Andy's. [74]They were looked at as stereotypes that reflected the racism of Whites. In the 1960's, Perry found favor with Cassius Clay who later became Muhammad Ali. At the time, Clay was a symbol for success to Black America. Clay became the heavy weight champion of the world, and he helped Perry financially.[75]

Some of Perry's roles in the films have been taken out of the picture because of the degrading image Stepin Fetchit represents to many Blacks.[76] Many of Perry's appearances in mainstream movies typically are cut out of the picture, regardless of the storyline. Prior to his death, he got back into the movie industry and appeared in Mom's Mabley comedy *Amazing Grace* in 1974, in which he scolded a White train conductor, lest he mistreat Moms.[77]

Later in his life, he received honor for being a trail blazer for Black actors and those in show business. In addition, he received an award from the NAACP and was elected into the Black Filmmaker's Hall of Fame in 1978.[78]

Chapter 8

Jack Johnson
– Leaves His Mark on Dad –

Heavy Weight Champion of the World: Jack Johnson [79]

Jack Arthur Johnson was born March 31, 1878. During his time, he was the Heavyweight Champion of the World[80] and known as the Galveston Giant. His roots were in Galveston, Texas.[81] He was America's best during his time. Johnson was the first Black and Texan[82] to win the title of the Heavy Weight Champion of the World.[83] He held the title from 1908-1915.[84]

According to Ken Burns, Johnson was one of the most famous and notorious African-Americans on earth. Dad also states he was pretty rowdy. He learned that after being cut in the face by Johnson. "Yes, he was a character," Dad remembers.

Johnson was the connoisseur at the Apex Club in Los Angeles, California. One night while Dad was in the club, one of the ladies had differences with Johnson. Johnson threw a wine glass and hit her in the head, and the glass broke and a piece of the glass hit Dad while he was on the dance floor with his girlfriend. He was hit in the head above his right eye. His eye was bleeding and the ambulance came and took both of them to the hospital. Dad gave up partying for the night and the lady continued partying like they did in Johnson's Club in Harlem. To this day the scar is still visible above Dad's right eye.

Johnson sold his club in Harlem in 1923 to a new owner name Madden who later called it The Cotton Club. When Johnson was the owner the club was a supper club, called Club Deluxe. It was located at 142nd Street and Lenox Ave.[85] He had opened his club and tried new ventures after his career in boxing. Johnson was an amateur cellist and bull-fiddler who was a connoisseur of Harlem night and now he was in Los Angles with his ideas at Apex Club. He also lectured, sold stocks, and worked as a movie extra.[86]

Johnson was 6 feet, 1 1/4 inches. He was a large man. He spent a lot of his time with older fighters in Boston, Chicago, and New York. He moved to California in 1901. Johnson became the "Black Heavyweight Champion of the World"[87] on February 3, 1903, in Los Angeles, California.[88] He fought Denver Ed Martin with a 20-round decision.

Johnson's mother and father were former slaves. He was the second child and first son of Henry and Tina "Tiny" Johnson.[89] Both of them were hard workers with minimum pay, but they were able to raise six children. They had nine children total and an adopted son.[90] Jack Johnson was literate and had five years of education. He was disbanded from the church because he did not believe God existed

Johnson fighting records are phenomenal. When he was fifteen years old he fought sixteen rounds and won the fight. In approximately 1897 when he was nineteen he began to get paid for fights. You could watch the fights in private clubs and other venues. When he was about twenty-three he was getting paid very well. Joe Chovnski trained Johnson in Galveston, Texas. He was a Jewish boxer who was small but in the heavy weight division. Choynski was experienced in his boxing career. Burns states, "Choynski knocked Johnson out in round three and the two were arrested for 'engaging in an illegal contest' and put in jail for 23 days."[91] America has always loved the sports of boxing, baseball, and horse racing. During this time in history boxing was illegal in most states, including Texas. The training began in jail with Choynski and Johnson. [92]

Johnson was on his way to be one of the greatest boxers of all time. His style was distinctive. He would be more on the defense; he would wait on a mistake from his opponent. Once he saw the weakness in his opponent, he would take advantage of the situation. He was very deliberate in his moves and would take his time and build himself up to be a more deliberate fighter. His ultimate goals were to win, knock his opponent out, and penalize him. He would avoid their punches, but he would come back with fast counter actions.[93] If he was pushed or backed up in a corner, he would respond with counter actions that were quick, intentional and powerful.[94]

Johnson's techniques were what made him the best. Many newspapers and reporters looked at his method of fighting as afraid to face or attack his opponent. They would report that he was sneaky, tricky and deceitful in his deliberations. On the other hand, Jim Corbett, a White fighter, used similar techniques, but was viewed as the best man in boxing.[95] Johnson had to deal with the rejection and segregation issues of his time.

It was calculated in 1902 that Johnson had won approximately 50 fights against both White and Black opponents. In 1903 he fought "Denver" Ed Martin for the World Black Heavyweight Championship. [96]James J. Jeffries refused to fight Johnson. Therefore if there was not a fight, he could not be the world champion.

According to Burns, "Blacks could not fight Whites in other arenas, but the heavyweight championship was such a respected and coveted position in America that Blacks were not deemed worthy to compete for it."

Johnson went on to fight former champion Bob Fitzsimmons in July 1907, and knocked him out in two rounds. He eventually won the World Heavyweight Title on December 26, 1908 when he fought the Canadian world champion Tommy Burns in Sydney, Australia, after following him all over the world, taunting him in the press for a match.[97] The fight lasted fourteen rounds before being stopped by the police in front of over 20,000 spectators. The title was awarded to Johnson on a referee's decision as a T.K.O, but he had severely beaten the champion.

During the match, Johnson had ridiculed Burns and his colleagues. When Burns was about to fall down, Johnson would keep him up and hit him and hold him up again, chastising him more. The event was being filmed and the camera was stopped just as Johnson was concluding the fight, so there would be no sign of Burn's conquer.

Shortly after Johnson won the fight with Burns, there was racial hostility because of Johnson's win. [98]There was a socialist named Jack London who wanted Johnson defeated.[99]

Hatred was rampart. People began to look for what was coined as the "The Great White Hope." This person would take the title away from Johnson. As the new title holder, all the White men that Johnson had to fight were categorized as "The Great White Hope." In 1909, he beat Victor McLaglen, Frank Moran, Tony Ross, Al Kaufman, and the middleweight champion Stanley Ketchel. The match with Ketchel was keenly fought by both men until the 12th and last round, when Ketchel threw a right to Johnson's head, knocking him down. Johnson got up very slowly and threw a straight and hit Ketchel in the jaw. Johnson knocked Ketchel out along with several of his teeth. His fight with "Philadelphia" Jack O'Brien was a disappointing one for Johnson: though scaling 205 pounds to O'Brien's 161, he could only achieve a six-round draw with the great middleweight.

The *"Fight of the Century"*[100] *Johnson and Jeffries, 1910*

James J. Jeffries, a former heavyweight champion, came out of retirement in 1910.[101] Jeffries came out of retirement because he wanted notoriety and to stand up for his race. He believed a White man was better than a Black man. Jeffries had been retired for six years and had to lose about 100 pounds to qualify for the correct fighting weight.

On July 4, 1910 there were about 22,000 people who attended. The arena was built in Reno, Nevada. [102]The ringside band played a song called "All coons look alike to me." The racial tension was high at this fight of the century.[103] The people who did the marketing for the fight told all the Whites to chant "Kill the nigger." Johnson was in better shape, and proved stronger and quicker than Jeffries. Jeffries was knocked down twice in the 15th round. In the history of Jeffries, this was the first time he had been knocked down twice in his vocation. Johnson was not allowed to knock him out.

The "Fight of the Century" [104]earned Johnson $225,000 and silenced the critics, who had belittled Johnson's previous victory over Tommy Burns as "empty," claiming that Burns was a false champion since Jeffries had retired undefeated.[105]

Riots and Aftermath

When Johnson won the fight, the jealousy was at the fore front. Several race riots started all over the United States. On July the fourth the outcome of the fight was proclaimed across the United States. People in New York, Washington D.C., Texas, and Colorado heard the stories. Many Whites were disappointed that Jeffries was defeated. They had lost their hope. Many Whites felt embarrassed because they felt the White race had been affected. Many were angry by Johnson's remarks of how great he was.

On the other hand, Blacks were ecstatic and proclaimed Johnson's great win as a victory for Blacks. In the eyes of Blacks, since he won, they won. William Waring Cuney was inspired to write the poem, "My Lord, What a Morning." This poem was written as a direct result of the response of Blacks after the great win by Johnson.

All over the United States, Blacks celebrated and on the spur of the moment they had prayer meetings and parades. Some of them purchased merchandise with the money they got from betting on the fight. Many Whites were angry and bitter and became incensed and riots broke out. The Blacks were simply rejoicing in the streets.[106] In some places the festivities were allowed. It was reported that the police officers in Chicago let the Blacks continue their celebration. In other cities, bitter and disgruntled Whites tried to stop the festivities. Many Blacks were attacked on the streets, and in some cases, gangs of Whites entered Black neighborhoods and tried to burn down apartment buildings. Police interrupted several attempted lynchings.

It was reported that more than 25 states and 50 cities had riots. Hundreds of Black people were injured and at least 23 Blacks and two Whites died in the riots. Reports indicate that a few Whites were injured when they tried to help the Blacks and stop the Whites from beating a Black man.

Due to the response of the fight, some states did not allow Johnson's victories over Whites to be filmed. [107]Black newspapers stated that White people did not like the fact of papers being circulated that had images of Blacks dominating Whites.[108] The papers said they allowed lynching to occur without criticism but did not want to show Johnson defeating a White man in a boxing arena. The Washington Bee wrote, "The White man cannot expect always to be in the front rank without competition, and we all should look at things this way."

In April of 1915 Johnson was knocked out and lost his title to Jess Willard.[109] Willard was a strong man and a working cowboy who did not start boxing until he was almost thirty years old. The fight was in Vedado Racetrack in Havana, Cuba. Over 25,000 people were in attendance. Johnson went down in the 26th round of the scheduled 45-round fight. Johnson found out he could not knock out Willard, who was

Jack Johnson, 1915. Library of Congress [110]

a counter puncher. Johnson was hurt from all of the heavy punches and was knocked out before the 26th round.

Johnson was considered one of the first famous black athletes. He was always in the press, on the radio, or in a movie.[111] Johnson made a lot of money doing advertising for different products, including patent medicines. He spent his money on things he liked, such as automobile racing and tailored clothes. Dad said he was nicely dressed.

He was a Black man who defied odds. He had a lot of jewelry and fine furs for his wives. It was stated that when he was stopped by a police officer for speeding, a ticket that cost $50, Johnson gave the officer a $100 bill and told him to keep the change because he would be coming back at the same speed. He liked opera and history. He admired Napoleon Bonaparte because he thought they had similar backgrounds.

Johnson went to several conventions regarding the social and economic "place" of Blacks throughout the United States. He married two White women in late 1910 or early 1911—the first was Etta Duryea.[112] She committed suicide in September of 1911 and Johnson quickly remarried to Lucille Cameron who was his bookkeeper.[113] The fact that both women were White caused considerable controversy at the time. [114]After he was married the second time, two ministers in the south recommended that Johnson be lynched. They both went to Canada and on to France soon after their marriage to escape criminal charges in the U.S.[115] He is mostly remembered for a glitzy life and controversy. In 1954 he was entered into the Ring Boxers Hall of Fame and the International Boxers Hall of Fame in 1990.[116]

Prison Sentence

Johnson began to fight in Mexico. He fought several fights in Mexico and later returned to the United States. In July 1920 Johnson turned himself in to the Federal Authorities. He was accused of violating the Mann Act.[117] The Mann Act is based on the following statue:

> **Whoever knowingly transports any individual in interstate or foreign commerce, or in any Territory or Possession of the United States, with intent that such individual engage in prostitution, or in any sexual activity for which any person can be charged with a criminal offense, shall be fined under this title or imprisoned not more than five years, or both HISTORY; ANCILLARY LAWS AND DIRECTIVES PRIOR LAW AND REVISION: 1948 Act: This section is based on Act June 25, 1910, ch 395, @@ 1, 2, 5, 8, 36 Stat. 825--827 (former 18 U.S.C. @@ 397, 398, 401, and 404).**

This law stopped Johnson from transporting women across state lines for prostitution and immoral purposes.[118] He sent his White girlfriend, Belle Schreiber, a railroad ticket to travel from Pittsburgh to Chicago. His criminal charges were based on his misuse of women, and he was cited for trafficking prostitution. Johnson served a one year sentence in the United States Penitentiary, Leavenworth.[119] In July of 1921, he was released. While in jail Johnson patented the wrench that would tighten and loosen. His modification of the wrench was US patent 1,413,121.[120]

Cameron divorced him in 1924 on the grounds of infidelity. Johnson then married an old friend, Irene Pineau, in 1925; she outlived him. Johnson had no children. In 1928, as he was getting older he had more losses and began to do exhibition bouts. Johnson died June 10 1946 when he was 68. He died near Raleigh, North Carolina.[121] The night he died he left a dinner angry after a racist incident. He drove his car around a bend too fast causing the car to lose control and wreck. The crash proved fatal.[122] He died one year before Jackie Robinson broke the "color line" in Major League Baseball. Johnson was buried in Graceland Cemetery in Chicago next to Etta Duryea. The grave has Johnson above the plot that stands above two of his wives. His grave is not marked Jack Johnson—only Johnson. His famous saying was "I'm Jack Johnson the Heavyweight Champion of the World. I'm Black. They never let me forget it. I'm Black all right! I'll never let them forget it!" Dad remembers the days of Jack Johnson and how he not only left his mark on him, but on the whole world.

Chapter 9

– Dad Goes to Jail During Prohibition –

History of Prohibition

Prohibition of alcohol, often shortened to the term "prohibition," was also known as Dry Law and refers to a law that prohibits alcohol in a given jurisdiction.[123] Prohibition in the United States was a measure designed to reduce drinking. Businesses that manufactured, distributed, imported, export or sold alcoholic beverages were closed.[124] The term can also apply to the periods in the history of the country during which the prohibition of alcohol was enforced. The leaders of the prohibition movement had a concern because Americans were drinking heavy. They were concerned that the European culture and the continuing immigration from Europe was spreading.[125] In the Muslim World, consumption of alcoholic beverages is forbidden according to Islamic Law.[126] The prohibition or "dry" movement began in the 1840's. Many religious denominations, especially the Methodists, helped to spearhead the movement.[127] Abstinence was the goal for everyone including institutions and anything that related to alcohol consumption. Preachers, such as Reverend Mark A. Matthews, linked liquor-dispensing saloons with prostitution.[128]

Some positive reports were registered in the 1850's, including Maine's total ban on the manufacture and sale of liquor, adopted in 1851.[129] The prohibition movement lost strength. Things weakened during the American Civil War (1861-1865) but revived in the 1880's. The Woman's Christian Temperance Union and the Prohibition Party were instrumental in the changes.[130] The Women's Christian Temperance Union was founded in 1873 and promoted prohibition rather than temperance.[131] Their preventative strategy was to educate the youth. It was believed that if it could "get to the children" it could create a dry sentiment leading to prohibition.

Kansas became the first state to outlaw alcoholic beverages in its constitution in 1881.[132] Carrie Nation received notoriety when she walked into saloons, scolding customers, and using her hatchet to destroy bottles of liquor.[133] Other activists enforced the cause by entering saloons, singing, praying, and urging saloon keepers to stop selling alcohol. Several other states and counties, mostly in the South, also enacted prohibition. The saloons and their political influence were characteristic of the time period. The anti-German mood of World War I supported the Anti-Saloon League through intense lobbying pushed the Constitutional amendment through Congress and the states, taking effect in 1920.[134]

Prohibition was an important force in state and local politics from the 1840's through the 1930's. The political forces involved were ethno-religious in character, as demonstrated by numerous historical studies. Prohibition was demanded by the "dries" they consisted of Protestants, particularly Methodists, Northern Baptists, Southern Baptists, Presbyterians, Disciples, Congregationalists, Quakers, and Scandinavian Lutherans. Saloons were looked at as politically corrupt and drinking as a personal sin. They were opposed by the "wets." They were Protestants (Episcopalians, German Lutherans) and Roman Catholics, who did not like the idea that the government should state what morality is.[135]

In New York City the wet stronghold was an active prohibition movement. The African American labor unions believed the workers would be more productive if they did not drink. In addition, Norwegian church groups believed that prohibition would benefit workers. Tea merchants and soda fountain manufacturers were in favor of prohibition because it could possibly increase their sales.

Eighteenth Amendment to the United States Constitution was established on January 16, 1920.[136] The new U.S. Constitution took away license to do business from the brewers, distillers, vintners, and the wholesale and retail sellers of alcoholic beverages.[137] The leaders of the prohibition movement were alarmed at the drinking behavior of Americans. Prohibition began on January 16, 1920, when the Eighteenth Amendment went into effect. [138]Federal prohibition agents [police] were given the task of enforcing the law. The accomplishments of prohibition were made by members of the Republican Party, the Democratic Party, and the Prohibition Party. The parties came together to make prohibition possible. National prohibition was accomplished by means of the Eighteenth Amendment to the United States Constitution (ratified January 29, 1919) and the Volstead Act (passed October 28, 1919).[139] The main forces were Protestants, who comprised majorities in the Republican Party in the North, and the Democratic Party in the South. Catholics and Germans were the main detractors; however, Germans were discredited by World War I, and their protests were ignored.

The 65th Congress met in 1917, and the Democratic dries outnumbered the wets by 140 to 64, while Republicans dries outnumbered the wets 138 to 62. In the 1916 presidential election, both Democratic incumbent Woodrow Wilson and Republican candidate Charles Evans Hughes ignored the prohibition issue, as was the case with both party's political platforms.

Both Democrats and Republicans had strong wet and dry factions, and the election was expected to be close, with neither candidate wanting to alienate any part of their political base.[140]

Although it was highly controversial, prohibition was widely supported by diverse groups. Progressives believed that it would improve society and the Ku Klux Klan strongly supported its strict enforcement as generally did women, Southerners, those living in rural areas, and African-Americans.[141]

While the manufacture, sale, and transport of alcohol were illegal in the U.S., it was not illegal in surrounding countries.[142] Distilleries and breweries in Canada, Mexico, and the Caribbean flourished as their products were either consumed by visiting Americans or illegally imported to the U.S. Chicago became known notoriously as a haven for disobeying prohibition during the time known as the Roaring Twenties.[143] Many of Chicago's most notorious gangsters, including Al Capone and his enemy Bugs Moran, made millions of dollars through illegal alcohol sales. Numerous other crimes, including theft and murder, were directly linked to criminal activities in Chicago and elsewhere in violation of prohibition.[144]

As prohibition became increasingly unpopular, especially in the big cities, "Repeal" was eagerly anticipated. On March 23, 1933, President Franklin

Roosevelt signed into law an amendment to the Volstead Act known as the Cullen-Harrison bill allowing the manufacture and sale of "3.2 beer" (3.2% alcohol by weight, approximately 4% alcohol by volume) and light wines. The Eighteenth Amendment was repealed later in 1933 with ratification of the Twenty-first Amendment, on December 5.[145]

The Twenty-first Amendment explicitly gives states the right to restrict or ban the purchase or sale of alcohol; this has led to a patchwork of laws, in which alcohol may be legally sold in some but not all towns or counties within a particular state. After the repeal of the national constitutional amendment, some states continued to enforce prohibition laws. Mississippi, which had made alcohol illegal in 1907, was the last state to repeal prohibition, in 1966. Kansas did not allow sale of liquor "by the drink" (on-premises) until 1987. There are numerous "dry" counties or towns where no liquor is sold; even though liquor can be brought in for private consumption.

Many social problems were acclaimed to prohibition period. The black market flourished and gangs took over the market. The gangs began to smuggle in stronger proof alcohol. The budget was $500 million a year nationwide to enforce the law of alcohol prohibition.

When repeal of prohibition occurred in 1933, organized crime lost nearly all of its black market alcohol profits

in most states (states still had the right to enforce their own laws concerning alcohol consumption), because of competition with low-priced alcohol sales at legal liquor stores.[146]

National prohibition of alcohol was from 1920 to 1933. Some looked at it as an experiment that was detrimental to society. "The objective was to reduce crime and corruption, solve social problems, reduce the tax burden created by prisons and poorhouses, and improve health and hygiene in America."[147] Once Prohibition ended half of the breweries reopened. The period afterwards opened up an industry for beer sales. Wine historians also note that prohibition destroyed what was a fledgling wine industry in the United States. Productive wine quality grape vines were replaced by lower quality vines growing thicker skinned grapes that could be more easily transported. Much of the institutional knowledge was also lost as wine makers either immigrated to other wine producing countries or left the business altogether.

Thirty six states were needed to pass the Amendment, but all thirty eight states that decided to hold conventions passed the Amendment. That was three fourths of the 48 that existed. Therefore, if Utah had not passed the law it still would have been promulgated. Despite the efforts of Heber J. Grant and the Latter Day Saints Church, a Utah convention helped ratify the 21st Amendment.[148] Utah can be considered the deciding 36th state to approve the 21st

Amendment and make it law and the day Utah passed the Amendment, both Pennsylvania and Ohio passed it as well.[149]

At the end of prohibition some supporters openly admitted its failure. A quote from a letter, written in 1932 by wealthy industrialist John D. Rockefeller, Jr., states:

> **When prohibition was introduced, I hoped that it would be widely supported by public opinion and the day would soon come when the evil effects of alcohol would be recognized. I have slowly and reluctantly come to believe that this has not been the result. Instead, drinking has generally increased; the speakeasy has replaced the saloon; a vast army of lawbreakers has appeared; many of our best citizens have openly ignored prohibition; respect for the law has been greatly lessened; and crime has increased to a level never seen before.**

Dad Goes to Jail

When Dad was a young man he learned many things in Tulsa about making corn whiskey and chock beer. While he was in California, he let his acquaintances know he was the man for the job because he had done the same thing on the infamous street on Greenwood—The Black Wall Street.

Dad resumed producing and distributing liquor in Los Angeles. He had several friends he would buddy with, and he began to do big business and sell liquor out of a Sommersville Hotel room on Central Avenue. One of the nightclubs he went to was Apex Night Club. Many theater folks, gamblers, and pimps hung around. Dad said "I suffered the consequences of not doing things for God and I was on the losing side." He ended up being told on and went to the Los Angeles county jail for bootlegging. During this time in history, it was against the law to sell or drink alcohol. Just think of how many people you know directly or indirectly who have been affected negatively by alcohol and tobacco.

Dad stayed in the Sommerville Hotel and knew the owners. This hotel was built by Dr. J.A. Sommerville in 1928. African-Americans called this their hotel. The NAACP had their first national meeting in the hotel.[150] When America experienced the great stock market crash of 1929, this hotel was sold and renamed the Dunbar Hotel by the new owners. Blacks were blessed to call the Sommerville their hotel.

Dad met many famous people in what he calls the sporting world. Jack Johnson, Cab Calloway, Duke Ellington, and Count Basic often frequented the famous Sommerville Hotel. According to Beverly Mateer Taylor, Sommerville went on to become a professional businessman and was a delegate to the California Democratic National Convention (1936) and became a part of the Los Angeles Police Commission (1949).[151]

Dad was in the Sommersville Hotel on the 4th floor at 400 block of South Central Ave when he got a knock on the door. He opened the door and a Black Los Angeles County Sheriff was there. He came into the room and began to search for whiskey. He found the whiskey that Dad had hidden. He told Dad he was under arrest for violating prohibition. He took Dad to the Los Angeles County Jail, and he was booked.

While Dad was in jail, he had a beautiful dream. He was on his bunk one night in prison, discouraged because his friends did not come to see him. They were running around at all the hotel and nightclubs, living the "high life." He felt defeated, down, and out. A group of people came to the jail from the Salvation Army. The first Sunday that they stopped by, Dad ignored the message of salvation and did not want to give up the world and all his worldly friends.

The next Sunday, he was discouraged even more and felt all alone because not one friend came to visit him. They promised him a visit and cigars while in jail. It was at his low point that he knew he needed a Savior. When the altar call went forth, he gave his heart to Jesus Christ. He had a beautiful dream that night and a wonderful vision from God. He flew over a green pasture for miles and miles and he could see beautiful flourishing trees and flowers. As he was in the air, he saw a great gulf between him and his grandmother,

mother, and others. He went so far but he could not go any further. He heard a voice say, "Between you and them is a great gulf. Go back and tell others about my loving kindness and mercy." Dad looked at this experience as the call God had for him to tell others to follow God and His Son Jesus.

While in jail, Dad notified his father of his conviction and his father got him a lawyer. The judge sentenced Dad to three to five years in jail. Dad left the Los Angeles county jail in 90 days. His significantly reduced sentence and favor with the judge showed Dad of God's amazing grace. This was the start of a brand new life in Christ.

Chapter 10

– Dad's Evangelistic Beginnings –

Emma Cotton

Dad was introduced to Emma Cotton. He rented from Mother Cotton before he moved to Chicago. He was under her covering a few years after Seymour's death. He traveled with her for a few years as an evangelist and helper.

Dad went to Aimee Semple McPherson's church with Mother Cotton on several occasions. McPherson is the founder of the International Church of Foursquare Gospel. She was a powerful woman of God. Dad received a white rose from her, as was her custom. She was born in 1890 and died in 1944.[152] Listed below is one of her writings which mirror Dad's life, prayers, and thoughts.

"You don't need to be an orator. What God wants is plain people with the Good News in their hearts who are willing to go and tell it to others. The love of winning souls for Jesus Christ sets a fire burning in one's bones. Soul winning is the most important thing in the world. All I have is on the altar for the Lord, and while I have my life and strength, I will put my whole being into the carrying out of this Great Commission."[153]

McPherson preaches to assemblage at Angelus Temple and to radio listeners. [154]

The dictionary of Pentecostal and Charismatic Movements says that she was "undoubtedly the most prominent woman leader Pentecostalism has produced to date." Many other women pioneers existed. Many of these women were pastors of Foursquare churches and patterned their ministries after McPherson. Cotton was a Black evangelist who was born in 1877 and died in 1952.[155] Cotton was mentored and inspired by McPherson to open the Azusa Temple in Los Angeles.[156] Cotton and her husband Henry were co-pastors of the church. Dad said that Henry worked for the railroad and did not travel as much during a season in his life. Later the Cotton's became associated with the Church of God in Christ. Today the church is known as the Crouch Memorial Church.

Dad states, "Cotton received the baptism of the Holy Spirit at the Azusa Mission and told me and others about the experience." She believed tongues were associated with the baptism of the Spirit as a doctrinal principle. Cotton sang, preached, and rejoiced freely in the Spirit. She was a respected Black pastor who established several churches in California. Many people were saved, and baptized with the Holy Spirit under her ministry.

She relayed that Seymour was the nominal leader of Azusa and that he usually kept his head inside the top of his two shoeboxes during the meetings while interceding. Cotton said, "Sometimes the enemy would come in and bind the services and some of the women would pray and intercede for the meetings until the services were freed." Cotton told testimonies of the events to Dad and others. She said, "The meetings reported at the revival Seymour opened in Los Angeles were phenomenal and God's power was evident."

The Azusa Mission

The Azusa Street Mission[157]

Dad was given the power of attorney for the Azusa Mission by Bishop Driscol under the order of and at the home of Mother Emma Cotton. The mission traced its roots to 312 Azusa Street in Los Angeles, California. Dad visited the site with mother Cotton.

In 1906 on Azusa Street what was known as the Apostolic Faith Mission welcomed people from all over the world. People's lives were being shaken by God's Spirit and lives were changed. The manifestation of God's presence went all over the world as people were baptized in the Holy Spirit.

William J. Seymour is the founder of the Azusa Mission. He published a great newspaper called The Apostolic Faith. During this time the newspaper went all over the world and people came from everywhere to receive the baptism of the Holy Spirit. When ministers and others would come from all over the world, they would go back and spread the fire.

Founder of the Azusa Mission: William J. Seymour[158]

Several articles were written about this event in the Los Angeles Times and other newspapers.

Historically, Pentecostalism began on Azusa Street and the revival lasted continually for three years. Thousands of people were converted and Azusa Street touched many denominations and nominal Christians were filled with the Spirit.

Charles Mason founder of the Church of God in Christ received the Baptism of the Holy Spirit at Azusa. Clark served Bishop Charles H. Mason under the direction of Mother Coffey the General Church Mother of the Church of God in Christ. He would pick up Mason at the train station in Chicago, and tend to his needs.

Founder of the Church of God in Christ: Bishop Charles Mason[159]

The Church of God in Christ along with several other denominations such as The Assemblies of God, the Church of God and Gaston B. Cashwell was instrumental in Holiness churches becoming Pentecostal.

Dad's secret is he believes in signs and wonders and manifestations of the Holy Spirit. He is a sign and wonder and a modern day miracle. He believes we should praise God, prophesy, and speak in tongues and interpret. In addition, he believes in the five fold ministry, healing, and deliverance. The gifts are not just for some but for everyone.

Dad Leaves California

Dad was converted in jail and was baptized with water at Second Baptist Church in Los Angeles California. He dated Esther one of the pastors' daughters. Then went to Azusa and later he went to Bishop Samuel Crouches' church at 33rd and Compton.

Dad left California with one of the overseers of Wisconsin. They drove from California to Wisconsin in Dad's black Model T Ford sedan. The man he came with was a friend of Bishop Charles Mason. Dad met him in California at Bishop Samuel Crouches' Church. Dad worked in his church for about a year and did revivals in Beloit and surrounding areas.

Dad let one of the young preachers in Milwaukee have his Model T. Later he bought a 1929 Black Nash. Dad left Wisconsin and went to Chicago where his sister was. In 1933 the pastor was Overseer W.M. Roberts. Robert's church was at 4021 S. States Street in Chicago, Illinois. Dad was a young minister. Dad helped serve the pastor with the ministry of helps and during Sunday School.

Chapter 11

– Living in Chicago –

His secular job was working downtown in a shoe shine shop on Madison. Later Dad worked with a friend from his church who had a cleaning and tailoring business. Dad had the business with his partner. He went to church with Dad and his wife was a church missionary.

Dad met his first wife Martha Barber at Bishop W.M. Robert's church. They had a beautiful wedding. Mother Coffey the church mother of the Church of God in Christ at the time encouraged Dad to marry Martha Barber. Coffey opened up her beautiful home for the reception and the wedding took place in the church on Christmas Eve of 1933 at 409 South States Street in Chicago. Later, Martha and Bishop's daughter Kelley Roberts left for Africa to do missions work and Dad continued on in his evangelistic calling in the United States. He stayed in Chicago and continued to serve Bishop Roberts.

The Worlds Fair during the Great Depression

In 1929 Dad went through America's Great Depression. The stock market crashed and the depression ended in 1941 when America went into World War II. Dad always seems to be in the middle of things that are cutting edge. Dad and one of the ministers from Pastor Robert's church in Chicago went to the Century of Progress International

Chicago's World State Fair, 1933[160]

Exposition. Chicago celebrated its 100 years of statehood. Dad went to the exhibition and saw the advertisement where a man talked about the television coming out in two years.

Century of Progress World's Fair Poster, 1933 [161]

The theme of the fair was technological innovations. The motto was "Science Finds, Industry Applies, Man Conforms."[162] The fair was from 1933 to1934. The sky ride and a transporter bridge were great attractors. The ride was available to ride from one end of the fair to the other.

History of the Fair

In January 1928 the planning committee was organized as a not for profit corporation. The plan was to host a World's Fair in Chicago in 1933. They held the fair around South Park. It was near land and water as it was located by Lake Michigan around 12th to 38th Street.[163] It was on a landfill of 427 acres in Burnham Park. The fair started on May 27, 1933 and ended in October 1934. [164]

In 1893 there were photo electric cells and they were transformed into electrical energy which was transmitted to Chicago.[165] In 1932 Arcturus a star was chosen because its lights were formulated during the World's Columbian exposition in 1893.[166] The fair was opened when the lights were turned on with energy from the rays of the star.

The fair did well. It was supposed to open in May and end in November 1933. People began to purchase memberships. When people bought them they could have a certain amount of individuals who could attend the park. The membership sales were very productive and the fair was self supported. The government did not have to sponsor it at all.

Reports state that $800,000 was raised while the United States was ending its depression. [167]The day before the stock market crash a $10 million bond was issued for the fair. In 1933 half the notes had been retired and all the notes retired by the close of the fair in 1934.[168]

James Tuslow of Adam's Dictionary of American History states there were 48,769,227 visitors for the 170 days starting May 27, 1933 and 22,565,859 paid admissions; during the 163 days beginning May 26, 1934, there were 16,486,377; a total of 39,052,236. [169]This was the first time in American history that an international fair paid for itself.

The buildings at the fair had a theme. It was created like a "Rainbow City." During the World's Columbian Exposition in 1893 it was a "White City", Art Deco design and the Grecian aspect of the previous fair.[170]

Entertainers played a great role too—dancer Sally Rand, and future star Judy Garland and The Andrews Sisters performed just to name a few. Auto exhibits from different car manufacturers were a hit.

The fair had exhibits that would be offensive today. One exhibit was to gawk at little people. It was called "Midget City." In addition, exhibits included incubators with real babies and portraits of Blacks.

Several styles of dream cars were on exhibition. Many of which Dad owned. Cadillac, Nash, Lincoln, Lincoln Zephyr, Pierce Arrow, Silver Arrow, but the Packard won the show.

Century of Progress U.S. Air Mail Stamp, 1933 [171]

A German airship was part of the spectacular. The sight of the Graft Zeppelin upset some of the German American population because of Adolf Hitler. [172]

Mural General Exhibit 3rd Pavilion [173]

Other exhibits included the Homes of Tomorrow Exhibition; the emphasis was new building materials and model homes. The first Major League Baseball All Star Game at Comiskey

Park was in conjunction with the fair.[174] A Union Pacific Railroad exhibit with the streamlined train with record breaking speeds was popular too.

Dad Prepares to Go to Africa

Later on Dad was planning to go to Africa. He sold his seven-passenger black 1929 Nash car to one of the members of the church. Dad sold the car to get money to go to Africa. After he sold the car the church mothers decided to take the women only. So Dad took the money he made for the sale of the car and went to school at a White Assembly of God Church in Nashville, Tennessee. He stayed in the "dormitory for Coloreds." A Black lady took care of the business for the Blacks because of segregation. Dad went though ministry training. He left the school and went back to Chicago and went into the ministry.

Chapter 12

Dad Living

– Amongst the Movie Stars –

Los Angeles

Dad's second wife was Ann. When talking about her it seems as though we've touched a soft spot. When discussing this part of his life, he was slightly dismayed, maybe even heart broken. He knew his wife before the Tulsa Riot, and he went back to Tulsa and married her. After they married in Tulsa at a Baptist Church off of Greenwood they went to Los Angeles together.

Before moving to California, Ann worked in south Tulsa in a home as a cook. They went to Los Angeles with great dreams for a happy future. When they arrived in Los Angeles, she got a job working for a wealthy doctor who was also a politician. Dad was his driver and she did the cooking. She was a great cook.

After they moved to Los Angeles, his wife wanted her mother to be with her. Dad drove back to Tulsa by himself. He picked up her mother who he called Mother Covington and took her to Los Angeles. Mother Covington was a missionary and a member of The Church of God in Christ. Dad's father Henry bought a house on the 200 block of Bonnie Brae Street. Dad and Ann moved in the house and Mother Covington lived with them once she got to Los Angeles. Ann looked for another job. She and Dad were hired by Joan Crawford.

Dad and Ann moved to Brentwood, California into Joan Crawford's home. Ann his wife was the cook and Dad was the butler or house man. They lived in Crawford's mansion up stairs where they had one room. They ate at the table after her and the guests. Dad called her Mrs. Crawford. Behind Crawford's home was a movie theatre. Crawford and her guest would watch movies. Dad would go into the movie theater to keep things clean. He would also use the place as a place to pray. It was often empty. Dad said her car was a Cadillac Convertible. He would drive the car and take her dog Chico to the veterinarian and to the groomer. The dog was a white poodle.

Crawford's who real name was Lucille Fay LeSuer;[175] was born March 23, 1905 and died May 10, 1977.[176] She was an

Academy Award winning actress. She was ranked at number ten for the greatest female stars of all time by the American Film Institute.[177] Crawford started out dancing on a motion picture contract with Metro Goldwyn Mayer Studios in 1925.[178] In the late 1920's she became more popular.

Dad and Crawford lived in two different worlds at the time, but their lives parallel in many ways. Dad and Crawford were close in age. Their family backgrounds both started in Texas. Crawford's father was reported to have abandoned the family in Texas. Crawford stated that she had been only a few months old when her father left. [179] Henry J. Cassin became her step-father while the family lived in Oklahoma. Crawford had her roots in Lawton, Oklahoma [180]and Dad was in Tulsa, Oklahoma.

The Comanche County Oklahoma census recorded Henry and Anna her mother living at 910 "D" Street in Lawton. [181]Crawford who was known as Lucille was five years old at the time and Dad, born in 1903, was seven years of age. Dad and Crawford were only two years apart. When she was young she went by the nickname "Billie." Is it any wonder that she had a theater in her home in California? She grew up watching vaudeville acts in Oklahoma at her stepfather's theater.[182] She was around several people who loved theatrics. Her ambition was to become a dancer.

When she was young she had three foot surgeries after she cut her foot on a milk bottle. After missing elementary school for a year and a half she was able to dance.[183] Around 1916, she moved to Kansas City, Missouri around the same time Dad was there with his father.[184] They were destined to meet. Later she went to college in Missouri, but academically she was not quite prepared. [185] She went to New York and danced in a chorus line. She still used the name Lucille LeSuer. In 1924 she signed her contract with Metro Golden Meyer[186] and moved to Culver City, California in January 1925.

Crawford started out in silent movies and eventually became known as Joan Crawford. A contest in one of the fan magazines selected her new stage name. A female entered the name Joan Crawford. She won $500 for the entry.[187]

Crawford did not like her name she thought it sounded too much like Crawfish. Later she accepted it. It was reported that Williams Haines an actor said, "You're lucky-they could have called you Cranberry and served you up with a Turkey!"[188]

Joan Crawford in, 1927 [189]

In the early thirties Crawford was teamed up with Clark Gable. During their time working together they started a relationship. It was stated that Louis B Mayer the Chief in the studio told Gable that the relationship would have to end. It was reported that Gable continued in his career. In addition, they meet privately for several years and in her later years she states the facts herself.[190]

She married Douglas Fairbanks in 1929.[191] He was her second husband. Crawford purchased a mansion at 426 North Bristol Avenue in Brentwood where Dad worked. The home was midway between Beverly Hills and the Pacific Ocean. This was her main home for the next 26 years.[192]

From the Trailer for The Women, 1939 [193]

Joan Crawford ,1948 [194]

In 1934 she did two movies *Chained* and *Forsaking All Others.* Crawford became a star at the box office.[195] Later, Crawford left MGM and signed with Warner Brothers. Crawford was also known for her time on television shows, radio programs, TV episodes and she did a pilot program called The Joan Crawford Show.[196]

Crawford later married Al Steele's. His company was Pepsi Cola.[197] After he died in 1959 she filled his vacancy. [198]Crawford received the bronze Pepsi bottle that was given away at the sixth annual Pally Award. This award was given to the person who made the greatest contribution to the company sales. Crawford retired from the company in 1973.[199] Crawford had five husbands: James Walton, Douglas Fairbanks Jr., Franchot Tone, Phillip Terry, and Alfred Steele.[200] Shortly after her last husbands death she sold her Brentwood mansion and stayed in New York until her death at age 72.

Crawford adopted five children but only raised four. Her five adopted children were Christina born in 1939, then Christopher born 1941 who was reclaimed by his mother, then she adopted another son and named him Christopher he was born in 1943,[201] Cynthia and Cathy were both born in 1947.[202]

Clark Gable

Dad served Clark Gable at Crawford's home. Dad would take his coat when he came over and tend to his needs. Then he and Ann served him at the table. Many times they would serve a three bone roast. Dad served him along with other stars like Charlie Chaplin.

Clark Gable's full name is William Clark Gable, born on February 1, 1901 and died on November 16, 1960.[203] Gable was named number seven of the Greatest Male Stars of All Time and was known as the King of Hollywood. In 1939 he was known for his role in the movie *Gone with the Wind*.[204]

Gable did not get his main start to become an actor until he was in his early twenties. He worked with small theater companies and went from the Midwest to Portland, Oregon.[205] He worked selling neck ties in Portland and met an actress named Laura Hope Crews. She inspired him to continue his career in theater. Another person who inspired him was Josephine Dillon.[206] She gave him some intense training, fixed his teeth, and helped him with preparations for a film career.[207]

Dillon became his manager after they went to Hollywood in 1924. She was seventeen years older than Gable, but she became his first wife. Over the next decade he was in several movies. In 1930 he divorced and married Ria Franklin Prentiss Lucas Langham. Things did not work out for them and he

Gable demonstrates the art of hitch-hiking in It Happened One Night, *1934* [209]

divorced her. [208] He signed with MGM. Later he became MGM's greatest star during the 1930's and 1940's.

From the Mutiny on the Bounty trailer, 1935 [210]

In 1939 he married Carole Lombard.[211] He was very happy at this time in his life. They had a ranch at Encino. In January 1942 Lombard was killed while on an airplane that crashed into a mountain near Las Vegas. He was devastated by this tragedy. Gable stayed at the ranch for the rest of his life, he made 27 movies and married twice more.[212]

World War II

Clark Gable with 8th AF in Britain, 1943 [213]

Gable joined the United States Army after Lombard's death. He was Captain Clark Gable and when he left the Army Air

Forces he was a major. He trained in the 351st Heavy Bomb Group. Gable went on five combat missions in England and earned an Air Medal and Distinguished Flying Cross.[214] Adolph Hitler admired Gable and offered a large amount of award money to any person who could capture him and bring him to him unharmed.[215]

Gable died November 1960 after his fourth heart attack. Many speculate the trigger for his heart attack being the movie he had recently completed that required him to be dragged by horses or the crash diets for movie roles. He was a heavy smoker and he was known to drink whiskey.[216]

Charlie Chaplin

Dad met another legend at Crawford's home. His name was Charlie Chaplain. Dad served him when he came to the house. He would listen to their interesting conversations around the dinner table while he was serving them. Chaplin was known for being non-conventional and non-conforming.

Chaplin was older than Crawford, Gable, and Dad. The three of them were born between 1901 and 1905; he was eleven to sixteen years older. He was born in 1889. His parents were music hall entertainers. His father died of alcoholism and mother had a mental breakdown because she could not find work.[217] Chaplin got his start in Sherlock Holmes production. He made slapstick films. His character was one of baggy pants, shoes on the wrong feet, black derby hat and tight frock coat.

Dad said Chaplin had opinions about taxes in America and many other things. He was known also to be a strong opponent of racism. In 1937 Chaplin decided to make a film on the dangers of repression. Chaplain states in his autobiography that people tried to stop the film *The Great Dictator* from being completed. Well, by the time the movie was finished, Britain was at war with Germany and the film was used as information against Hitler. [218]

J. Edgar Hoover and the Federal Bureau of Investigation had about 1,900 page file on his activities with politics. The Attorney General under Hoover's advice was told not to let Chaplin back into America after he had left.[219]

When Chaplin went to London in 1952 he was not allowed back into America to live. He was blacklisted from making films in Hollywood. In 1964 he wrote his autobiography and in 1972 he was invited back to the United State to receive a special award from the Academy of Motion Picture Arts and Sciences. He died December 25, 1977.[220]

Charlie Chaplin [221]

Chapter 13

Dad Goes Back to
– Oklahoma during World War II –

Dad and Ann left Joan Crawford's before she adopted her children. He and Ann went on to do other work after Ann and Crawford had a disagreement which was later resolved. Ann and Dad moved back to Bonnie Brae Street and later separated.

Dad went back to Oklahoma and worked in the Douglas Aircraft Plant. His department helped make parachutes and other departments helped make things for airplanes. Dad heard of the plant when an advertisement went out for people to work at the plant. This plant made important things for World War II.

One of the former employees gives her account as follows: "The bomber plant's 1.6 million square feet, buzzing with activity during World War II. You can't imagine how... you're an 18-year-old from a little, small town, and you're out there in that shop--I mean in the shop--and I'm trying to find my way out," Dollarhite recalled, sitting in her quiet south Tulsa home. [222]

"I'm standing in the middle of it, and I look down one way, and I look down the other way, and it's forever. And I thought, 'My gosh, what am I doing here?'" Dollarhite was one of thousands of "Rosie the Riveters" in Oklahoma who took jobs in defense plants during the war. Defense plants and military installations provided a major employment boost as the state recovered from the Dust Bowl years. [223]

When World War II loomed, Tulsa was struggling. It was reported that the city lost 12,000 adults between 1930 and 1940. According to historical reports, thousands of people did not have work, and there were about 2,000 vacant homes in Tulsa.[224] Later the Douglas Aircraft Plant built an assembly plant in Tulsa.[225] Residents passed a bond issue to buy up 1,100 acres of land for the plant's construction.

During 1941 and 1945, the Douglas plant took sub-assemblies from Ford Motor Co.'s Willow Run plant in Michigan and produced 962 B-24 bombers, 615 A-24 dive bombers and 1,343 A-26 attack bombers. A neighboring modification center installed nose guns on B-17s. [226]

During Douglas' best times, it employed about 23,000 people. In 1943, President Theodore Roosevelt came to Tulsa. President Roosevelt, arriving in a top-down, black convertible sedan, inspected the plant. Surprised workers stopped to cheer and greet him.[227]

In 1945, with the war ending, orders at the Douglas Aircraft Plant dwindled. About 7,500 workers, including Dollarhite, got their walking papers that year. Dad was one of the workers who had lost his job. Shortly afterwards he went back to California.

Dad's Family Life

Dad had a child name Marcie Dee. Dora Lee was her mother. They met in a town called Landon, California. They were in the Church of God in Christ. Later they separated because of her heavy drinking. Dad continued in the Church work and later she died. During the beginning of their marriage Dad worked at the Post Office in downtown Los Angeles while his child was a baby.

His last wife was Bessie Drake. They meet in Bakersfield, California. Bessie was a servant to Bishop Charles Mason and his wife, Elsie Mason. She was an awesome church worker. They worked together in ministry until her death.

After her death in the late seventies Dad continued on being a traveling evangelist. In 1990 Dad adopted Gwen Williams and Star Williams as his daughter and grand daughter. In 1992, Dad and Williams wrote a book titled, *The Azusa Mission*. They have traveled as an evangelistic team for the last fifteen years spreading the gospel of Jesus Christ and were pastors of a holiness work in Seattle, Washington for five years.

Chapter 14

– Dad The World Traveler –

Guys and Cars

Dad has always had a great love and appreciation for nice cars. The Cadillac is his favorite. A Model T Ford was Dad's first car. He bought it with the money he made from picking grapes in Delano, California. He purchased it in California and drove it to Chicago.

Ford Model T Coupe. Photo Credit Gary D. Avey [228]

Dad is a man of adventure. He has traveled the roads of America since 1921. In the 1930's, he sold his 1929 Nash to make a trip to Africa on which he did not get to go.

Dad is well known for driving from Tulsa, Oklahoma to California without stopping to sleep with his trusty bag of Fritos. The Fritos helped him stay awake while driving. Dad's last trip by himself to California was in 2001 when he was 98 years old. He drove to San Francisco to bury his

1918 Nash [229]

nephew Robert. On this last trip to California, Dad swung by Seattle, Washington to unsuccessfully apply for a passport. On the road trips he'd rarely stop to sleep, unless it was for a few minutes at a rest stop. Dad enjoys seeing the sights of the road, including the trees and the different landscapes. One of his main memories was going from gravel roads to paved highways.

Dad is a World Traveler

His idea of living is traveling around the world blessing people with the love of God. The spirit of Dad is free, independent and unencumbered. His life and joy comes from traveling, rather driving, flying, or sailing. He lights up at the idea of going somewhere.

In spite of his unsuccessful attempt to go to Africa in the 1930's, he made it in 2006 at the young age of 103 and returned for a second time in 2007. At 105, he plans to accompany the Life Enrichment Missions team to Guatemala in June 2008. You may think, 104 years old! Does he ever get tired? Well, the answer is no. He is such a go-getter. Sometimes we'll ask him if he's tired or needs some rest, and he'll say, "Tired? Tired of doing what?!" To Dad, ministry is his life, and he doesn't view it as work, but living. He loves to travel and always says that God called him as an evangelist—well, I think God knew what he was doing when he called him to be an evangelist. I suppose Dad is the oldest traveling evangelist in the world, amongst many other things.

While in Africa, Dad touched many lives for Christ. He loved people and shared Christ everywhere he went. "If you're on God's side you're a winner..." is his famous saying, and he shared it everywhere he went, "If you're on God's side, you're a winner. If you're not on God's side, you are a loser. Get on God's side!" His message carries simplicity and profoundness. Revelations 3:15-16 reinforces Dad's legendary words—"I know your deeds, that you are neither cold nor hot. I wish you were either one or the other! So, because you are lukewarm—neither hot nor cold—I am about to spit you out of my mouth. We must choose a side to be on—God's or Satan's side, the choice if yours.

Dad with Pastor Bonnie Deuschle of Celebration Ministries International-Zimbabwe Africa, 2007 [230]

Dad Clark at Celebration Ministries International-Zimbabwe, Africa, 2007. [231]

Dad Clark with young girl. She painted a picture for him. Zimbabwe, Africa, 2007. [232]

Dad Clark preaching in Zimbabwe, Africa, 2007. [233]

Dad Clark preaching in Zimbabwe, Africa, 2007. [234]

Dad Clark preaching in Zimbabwe, Africa, 2007. [235]

Dad Clark preaching in Zimbabwe, Africa, 2007.[236]

Dad Clark laying hands on every participant at the tent revival. Zimbabwe, Africa, 2007.[237]

Dad Clark kisses a baby. Zimbabwe, Africa, 2007.[238]

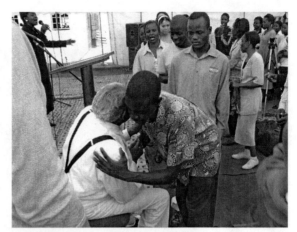

*He never
runs out
of kisses.
Zimbabwe,
Africa,
2007.*[239]

*He prays for
a young boy,
2007.*[240]

*Dad Clark
preaching in
Zimbabwe, Africa,
2007.*[241]

Dad Clark kissing an AIDS infected young boy. Zimbabwe, Africa, 2007.[242]

Chapter 15

– Dad's Secret to Long Life –

His Secret — Spiritually

Prayer and Fasting

We all know that for every born again Christian, prayer is an essential part of everyday life. The Apostle Paul beckons us in 1 Thessalonians 5:17 to pray continually. The more we pray the greater our relationship is with the Lord. The more intense our fellowship is with Christ the risen Savior the better our lives turn out. Jesus gives us two indispensable commandments in the Scriptures: love God, and love others. Dad is a man that truly loves God and others. He is a man that prays without ceasing. The basis for his prayer life is found in Matthew: But when you pray, go into your room, close the door and pray to your Father, who is unseen. Then your Father, who sees what is done in secret, will reward you (Matthew 6:6).

Dad is a man that knows how to touch the throne room of heaven. He is a man that has practiced prayer throughout his lifetime. Often when he prays, he lies prostrate on the floor before the Lord. Something is to be said about a man of God prostrate before God; it shows humility and submission before God. He is a man that follows the Holy Spirit. He is a modern day miracle because he chooses to simply believe and obey the Scriptures that say: Love God and Love Each Other. There is no magical formula to why he has lived to see 105 years old, except that he is in divine fellowship with his Creator everyday.

Many health benefits from prayer exist. Living longer, being healthier and having a positive outlook on life are just a few of those benefits, all of which Dad possess. However, experts back up what Christians have known for years regarding the health benefits of prayer. Many benefits of prayer exist and Clem Boyd sums those benefits up nicely:

Ever wonder how Methuselah lived to be almost 1,000 years old? Maybe he had a good prayer life. At least that's what a recent study from the Duke University Medical Center indicates. Looking at 4,000 older adults from rural North Carolina, the Duke team concluded that even occasional private prayer and Bible study helped people live healthier and longer lives. "This is one of the first studies showing that people who pray live longer," said researcher Harold Koenig. Dr. David Stevens, a family practitioner and executive director of the Christian Medical Association, said Christians shouldn't be surprised. "People who are anxious, worried and depressed do poorly when they're sick," Stevens said. "Those with hope and peace in the midst of a [health] struggle seem to do much better. People with religious commitments have that hope and peace." Prayer brings a definite physiological benefit, noted Dr. Bob Orr, director of clinical ethics at Fletcher Allen Health Care, the teaching hospital for the University of Vermont. "I certainly encourage people who are believers to pray," Orr said. "My observation is the person who prays is less stressed. He becomes less anxious, and his blood pressure and pulse improve." Stevens pointed to one study which showed the risk of diastolic hypertension was 40 percent lower among those who studied the Bible daily and attended church weekly. Another study concluded that elderly heart patients were 14 times less likely to die after surgery if they found comfort in religious faith. "This has an impact on longevity," Stevens said. "The overall life expectancy gap is seven years between those who go to church once a week versus those who don't attend at all. We will live longer if we have a strong faith.[243]"

Dad is a Man of Faith

The Bible says, "Without faith, it is impossible to please God, for he who comes to God must believe that He is God, and a rewarder of those who diligently seek Him" (Hebrews 11:6).

Therefore, expectation is the key to receiving from God when you pray. Jesus said in Mark 11:24, "Whatsoever things you desire when you pray, believe you receive them and you shall have them." Therefore, believe you receive when you pray. What good does it do to pray without expecting to receive? You might as well not pray at all, for faith is required to receiving what you desire.[244]

Dad agrees with Daniel Brown in his article *Without Faith It Is Impossible to Please God*, that God will do His part when we pray, but we must also do our part. Our part is simply to believe. So many people are busy asking God, but never really believing what they are praying for will come to pass. Dad believes when he prays for something to happen. You can tell by the way he talks, and acts.[245]

Most people have been raised to believe in a terrible outcome instead of a positive result, and actually, taught to believe in a negative conclusion. It's a safety mechanism that says, "Don't get your hopes up, so if it doesn't work out, you won't be disappointed."[246]

There's no logic in that because you will be disappointed anyway. Now, it's normal to feel disappointment. It's what you do with the feelings of disappointment that's important, but that's another subject.[247]

Believing in a positive outcome is vital to our success. If we could only believe that God has our best interest in mind and simply trust that everything will work out, we would see great results. Life would change in ways we'd never thought possible. But, most people just can't believe things will workout for them. They look at past results and judge their future based on their past.

It's a fact that the best predictor of future behavior, is past behavior. The good news is, that your behavior is a choice. Your past does not have to equal your future! Just change your expectations and have faith.[248]

James 2:20 tells us that "Faith without works is dead," which means "faith" is an action word. The word "faith" in Webster's Dictionary is also translated as "belief." So, believing is an action. And, it really doesn't take any more effort to believe than to not believe. It's just an attitude.

It's been said that if you truly believe in something (having faith that it will happen), then it really will happen. A lot of people don't completely accept that, but the Bible is clear; what you believe is what you get. Jesus said in Matthew 9:29, "According to your faith, let it be done unto you."[249]

He didn't say we would see the manifestation of our prayers immediately. We must keep believing and not waver: "For a man who wavers is like a wave of the sea driven with the wind and tossed. Let not that man think that he shall receive anything of the Lord" (James 1:6-7).

Expectation is the key to receiving from God when you pray! If you are not going to expect God to act, then don't pray at all. It's ineffective and displeases Him when you don't believe. Remember, Hebrews 11:6 says, "Without faith, it is impossible to please God." God will do His part when you pray, but only if, you do your part, and that is simply to believe.[250]

Dad Practices Listening, Meditation & Peace

He is a man of quietness and meditation which brings peace. Proverbs 14:20 says that a heart at peace gives life to the body. One look at Dad and you know he is a man of peace. With observation, Dad is a man of few words. He does not flaunt his knowledge and wisdom but primarily listens and meditates, unless he is asked a question. Something is to be said about listening more than talking. It's been said that we have one mouth and two ears; therefore we should listen twice as much as we talk. Think about the people in your life that tend to be good listeners rather than talkers—they seem calm, caring, pleasant and delightful to be around.

In addition to reading the Word of God, he also meditates on the word day and night. He is able to sit hours upon hours reading and studying the Word of God. He has hidden the Word in his heart that he might not sin against God (Psalms 1:2-3). As a result of years of meditating on God's Word, he is able to recall numerous Scriptures without effort and with application. Some of his favorite scriptures passages are, "Come unto me all ye that labor and are heavy laden, and I will give you rest" (Matthew 11:28); "For God so loved the world that he gave his only begotten son, that whosoever believeth in him shall not parish but have everlasting life" (John 3:16). The Prodigal Son that returns home (Luke 15). Be a hearer and doer of the word (James 1:22).

Dad is an Intercessor

Often Dad is found in his room praying for others: the needy, sinners, the homeless, the afflicted, and the poor. He has a heart for those that are less fortunate, and he realizes the power that prayer has to change their situation. Let us have a heart for the least of these.

Dad Talks with God

Dad has genuine conversations with God. He talks and walks with God. He constantly listens to God. Many nights I can hear him in his room talking to God as if He is right there in the room with him. Often he is on his knees too. Dad truly loves God with all his mind, body and spirit. I have observed that he lives his life to please the Lord. He could care less what people think of him, but highly esteems the opinion of God.

Dad realizes the importance of denying oneself the pleasures of this world for a season. At 105 years old, he still observes fasts for various reasons. Mainly to see sinners saved and revival in the church.

After Dad was converted in the city of Los Angeles, he ventured down to Delano, California, where he heard they made good money picking and cutting grapes. He claims he was quite a grape cutter. He would fill up the baskets and take them to the buyer to receive pay by weight. He learned to speak Spanish working with the Mexicans, although he has forgotten much of it. He worked in Delano for a while and even received gold back bills for picking and cutting grapes.

Once he was converted he believed that he could be like the apostles with fasting and prayer. Dad had a thirst for God that was unable to be quenched in the early 1920's. In the city of Delano, he prayed and fasted nearly two weeks and he was baptized in the Holy Ghost and spoke in tongues. The fast was miraculous because he went a full ten days without any food or water. Ever since the 1920's, Dad has been a man of intense prayer and fasting. He is a man that fasts regularly.

His Secret—Naturally

Dad's Eating Habits

Meat makes men strong. If you know anything about Dad, it's probably that his favorite food is meat—especially beef. He loves to cook a beef stew with garlic cloves, tomatoes, and potatoes. He lives off this stew when he cooks for himself. He is a generally healthy eater. Though many see him at restaurants eating steaks or hamburgers, they are not his main diet. For breakfast he usually eats steak and eggs or bacon and eggs.

Digestion starts in the mouth. He thoroughly chews his food—The rule is to chew each bite of food over 22 times. Dad probably chews his food over 30-40 times per bite. Chewing foods helps with digestion and when we chew more we feel fuller sooner. He picks teeth—After every meal, he picks his teeth. He always asks for a toothpick after every meal. He has all of his natural teeth because of special care he has given them.

Eat whatever is put before you. Dad is known for cleaning his plate completely, leaving nothing. He is neither a wasteful person nor picky person—he eats everything. Luke 10:8 states, "When you enter a town and are welcomed, eat what is set before you." When we went to Africa in 2007, he was the one that didn't get sick even though he didn't care about hand sanitizer or washing his hands profusely. He wasn't picky about the food but prayed over everything that was put before him. One man's faith allows him to eat everything, but another man, whose faith is weak, eats only vegetables. (Romans 14:2)

Don't forget to pray. First Thessalonians 5:16-17 tells us to be joyful always and to pray continually. Dad prays over his food in thanksgiving. He is grateful every time he has the opportunity to eat. His grateful heart and his prayer to the Lord—it's no wonder he can eat what he pleases. Even though he eats whatever he pleases, he makes healthy choices unless it is a special occasion; then he'll have a soda or may have a dessert. He is a man of moderation.

Dad is a man of moderation. Drastic measures aren't necessary when you practice moderation. This principle applies in eating, spending and relationships. Manage as you go through life, and you won't have to worry about losing weight or taking medications later on in life. Moderation is the key. Even the Bible tells us to do everything in moderation (Philippians 4:5, KJV)

Baths

Dad loves to take hot baths. He is a bath man. Now he doesn't take 1-2 baths a week, but 1-2 baths per day. He always takes baths and soaks for a long time. The fact that he can stop what he's doing and take a bath speaks to the serenity of his nature. Some experts have suggested that baths alone even lower blood pressure and more so with diet and exercise.

Suited Up

Dad has always been a fine dresser. We have tried our hardest to get him into more casual clothing, but to no avail. He thinks colored shirts are for working in the yard. White dress shirts are the only ones he'll wear. His shoes are strictly Stacey Adams, and most of the time he is in a two piece suit, if not a three piece suit.

Dad is Independent and Adventurous

Don't let his smooth demeanor fool you, because if he needs to patch up a few spots on a pair of pants, he can do that too. He is known for "tailoring" his own clothes. He will do anything from shorten his sleeves to widening his pants. Below are some of those moments. In these pictures he is patching his pajamas.

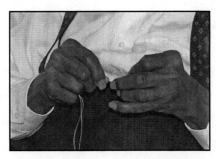

Dad threading his needle, 2007.[251]

First he threads his needle. It's amazing how nearly 105 year old hands can thread a needle! Many elderly people shake or have such bad arthritis that they can't hold still enough; this is a miracle.

He sews better than most. As you can see, he isn't afraid to do things for himself. Now you may think, "Why doesn't he buy new pajamas?" He has come through many wars, prohibition and the Great Depression, so being frugal and conservative is part of his makeup. He doesn't throw away clothes that can be repaired. He eats everything on his plate, no matter how much—you may have even witnessed him "dining sufficiently."

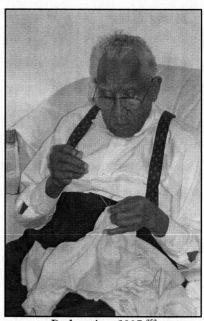

Dad sewing, 2007.[252]

Dad's Rollercoaster Ride

In the summer of 2000 a group of youth went to a local amusement park in Tulsa, Oklahoma. He often says he is "following the young folks." It is true—he literally follows the young folks! You may see Dad at the local roller skating rink, horse back riding, riding a bike, walking at the lake or on a rollercoaster in Tulsa, Oklahoma. Dad once rode the Zingo rollercoaster at Bells Amusement Park. We didn't actually think he would do it because it was, to me, an empty suggestion.

After he finished his hamburger, he said, "Where is it?" I said, "Where is what?" "The rollercoaster!" He proclaimed. So we all follow him reluctantly to the Zingo rollercoaster, and to our surprise, he rode it. And survived! The owner of the park was there to meet us as we exited the ride. He was so impressed with Dad that he invited us back to film a commercial for July 4th. So don't ever say, "I'm too old to ride a rollercoaster"—just think about 97 year old Dad and march on!

His Secret — Mentally

Dad has a No-Fail Mentality

Dad Clark has a no-fail mentality. If he sets his mind to do it, he will do it. He defines determination. We were ministering during a revival in 2006, and as we were leaving for the meeting, Dad throws up all over the yard of the guest house we were staying in. During that particular day, he was sick and throwing up several times. We encouraged him to stay home and rest, but he didn't want to hear that. He insisted on going to church. He said he wasn't going to let the devil defeat him. As we were driving to the meeting, he needed to throw up again. I stopped the car and he threw up again! With determination to forge forward he insisted we continue on to church. When we arrived at the church, he jumped energetically out of the car and marched up to the pulpit to take his place as main speaker. The message he ministered was one of his best messages ever. He preached with power and authority with no trace of fatigue or sickness. He signed autographs for many at the end of the evening and threw up again in the process. That was the first time I had known him to be sick.

If he wasn't so persistent, many lives wouldn't have been changed as they were changed that evening. He felt much better the next day though and has not been sick since then.

We rejoice in our sufferings, because we know that suffering produces perseverance; perseverance, character; and character, hope. And hope does not disappoint us, because God has poured out his love into our hearts by the Holy Spirit, whom he has given us.

If you've heard Dad read the Bible or speak, you know that he is very literate and articulate. Much of his knowledge was self taught and picked up through reading the Bible. He can spend hours upon hours reading the Word of God. He has a true hunger for the Lord; even at his mature age he longs for wisdom, knowledge, and understanding. When talking to Dad about childhood memories, he will remember the smallest details like street names, childhood teachers, and neighbors. It's no doubt the Lord has preserved his mind. Isaiah 26:3 says, "You will keep in perfect peace him whose mind is steadfast, because he trusts in you." Dad's mind is certainly in perfect peace.

Just For Fun

Things he's seen:

Born February 13, 1903

13 years 9 months older than Walter Cronkite, age 91

18 years 5 months older than Nancy Reagan, age 86

21 years 4 months older than George Herbert Bush, age 83

28 years 7 months older than Barbara Walters, age 76

30 years 9 months older than Larry King, age 74

37 years 0 months older than Ted Koppel, age 67

40 years 5 months older than Geraldo Rivera, age 64

43 years 5 months older than George W. Bush, age 61

48 years 5 months older than Jesse Ventura, age 56

52 years 8 months older than Bill Gates, age 52

57 years 6 months older than Cal Ripken Jr., age 47

63 years 5 months older than Mike Tyson, age 41

67 years 5 months older than Jennifer Lopez, age 37

72 years 11 months older than Tiger Woods, age 31

79 years 4 months older than Prince William, age 25

and he was:

98 years old at the time of the 9-11 attack on America

96 years old on the first day of Y2K

94 years old when Princess Diana was killed in a car crash

92 years old at the time of Oklahoma City bombing

91 years old when O. J. Simpson was charged with murder

90 years old at the time of the 93 bombing of the World Trade Center

87 years old when Operation Desert Storm began

86 years old during the fall of the Berlin Wall

82 years old when the space shuttle Challenger exploded

80 years old when Apple introduced the Macintosh

80 years old during Sally Ride's travel in space

78 years old when Pres. Reagan was shot by John Hinckley, Jr.

76 years old at the time the Iran hostage crisis began

73 years old on the U.S.'s bicentennial Fourth of July

71 years old when President Nixon left office

69 years old when Alabama Gov. George C. Wallace was shot

66 years old at the time the first man stepped on the moon

65 years old when Martin Luther King Jr was assassinated

62 years old during the Watts riot

60 years old at the time President Kennedy was assassinated

56 years old when Hawaii was admitted as 50th of the United States

54 years old when the Soviet satellite Sputnik 1 was launched

50 years old at the end of the Korean War

42 years old when the atomic bomb was dropped on Hiroshima

38 years old at the time of the Japanese attack on Pearl Harbor

31 years old in the year radar was invented

26 years old when the American stock market crashed

23 years old in the year of the first talking motion picture

12 years old at the time of the sinking of the Lusitania

11 years old when the First World War began

9 years old at the time of the maiden voyage of the Titanic

3 years old during the great San Francisco earthquake.[253]

Dad's Favorite Sayings

* The Big Boss upstairs (Is Jesus!)

* I have dined sufficiently, and that is without a shadow of a doubt

* Who said I wasn't going to make it

* All the way back (Dad uses this on elevators only to direct everyone to make room for others.)

* I'm following the young folks

- Little boy said...

- Don't start nothin'

- I don't know nothin'

- Mmm-huh

- That's a dirty shame

- Well, what do you know?

- The "G" is for Grandville

- Now wait a minute

- I stays ready

- Now whatcha gonna do about that

- Where's the beef?

- Don't hurt yourself (Don't eat too much)

- You sure are healthy looking (You are probably overweight and therefore unhealthy.)

- They were fat and fine like little pigs

- If you're on God's side you are a winner (Jesus is the only way to heaven)

- Get behind me Satan

If you have been personally touched by Dad's life and would like to financially support his ministry, bless his life, send him a birthday present for making it to 105 years old or send an encouraging word, please contact him and send all correspondence to:

Address: 2201 NW 122nd Street, Suite 409, Oklahoma City, OK 73120

Website: www.LifeEnrichmentInc.com

Telephone: 918-409-7700

If you would like to book Dad for a speaking engagement or event please call 918-409-7700.

To purchase additional copies of this book, please call 918/409.7700 or you may also purchase online at www. LifeEnrichmentInc.com

Endnotes

1   http://thinkexist.com/quotation/it_isn-t_what_you_have-or_who_
    you_are-or_where/204180.html

2   http://www.amazon.com/Tough-Minded-Tender-Hearted-People-
    Robert-Schuller/dp/0553247042

3   http://www.amazon.com/Tough-Minded-Tender-Hearted-People-
    Robert-Schuller/dp/0553247042

4   wikipedia.org/wiki/History_of_slavery_in_the_United_States

5   Ibid, p. 1

6   http://www.simplcom.ca/lnq/mlk3/blackslavery.html   Page   1
    Retrieved on 10-10-07

7   Otto H. Olsen (December 2004). Historians and the extent of
    slave ownership in the Southern United States. Civil War History.
    Southernhistory.net. Retrieved on 2007-11-23.

8   James M. McPherson (1996). *Drawn with the Sword: Reflections on
    the American Civil War*. New York: Oxford University Press, p. 15.

9   Weiss, T. "Review of Robert William Fogel and Stanley L.
    Engerman, *"Time on the Cross: The Economics of American Negro
    Slavery"*, *Economic History News Services - Book Reviews*, November
    16, 2001. Book review. Retrieved October 24, 2007.

10 www.memory.loc.gov/ammem/aap/timelin3.html p. 1

11 Ibid, p.1

12 Ibid, p. 1

13   www.ferris.edu/jimcrow/coon/p. 1

14   wikipedia.org/wiki/History_of_slavery_in_the_United_States

15   Ibid p. 1

16   www.infoplease.com/timelines/slavery.html

17   www.infoplease.com/timelines/slavery.html Page 1

18   www.hti.math.uh.edu/curriculum/units/2003/01/10/03.01.10. p. 1

19   Ibid

20   Ibid

21   www.klru.org/austinnow/archives/gentrification/index.asp p. 1

22   Ibid

23   klru.org/austinnow/archives/gentrification/index.asp p. 1

24   austintexas.org/visitors/insiders_guide/diverse_austin/african_
     american

25   klru.org/austinnow/archives/gentrification/index.asp p. 1

26   austintexas.org/visitors/insiders_guide/diverse_austin/african_
     american

27   Ibid

28   Ibid

29   austintexas.org/visitors/insiders_guide/diverse_austin/african_
     american

30   klru.org/austinnow/archives/gentrification/index.asp p. 1

31   Ibid

32   Ibid

33   Ibid

34   tsl.state.tx.us/governors/earlystate/pease-burleson.html

35   www.state.ok.us/osfdocs/stinfo2.html#AFRICAN%20AMERICANS
     Page 1

36   Ibid, p. 1

37   Ibid

38   Ibid

39   Ibid

40   http://www.cdc.gov/EPO/DPHSI/121hist.htm

41   Ibid, p. 1

42   http://www.rootsweb.com/~okgenweb/vital/info.htm

[43] Bob Hower. 1921 Tulsa Race Riot: Angels of Mercy. 2001

[44] Bob Hower. 1921 Tulsa Race Riot: Angels of Mercy. 2001

[45] Ibid

[46] Ibid

[47] Bob Hower. 1921 Tulsa Race Riot: Angels of Mercy. 2001

[48] Bob Hower. 1921 Tulsa Race Riot: Angels of Mercy. 2001

[49] Ibid

[50] Bob Hower. 1921 Tulsa Race Riot: Angels of Mercy. 2001

[51] Bob Hower. 1921 Tulsa Race Riot: Angels of Mercy. 2001

[52] Ibid

[53] Bob Hower. 1921 Tulsa Race Riot: Angels of Mercy. 2001

[54] Bob Hower. 1921 Tulsa Race Riot: Angels of Mercy. 2001

[55] Bob Hower. 1921 Tulsa Race Riot: Angels of Mercy. 2001

[56] Watkins, Mel, Stepin Fetchit, Life and Times of Lincoln Perry

[57] http://www.dougmacaulay.com/kingspud/sel_by_actor_index_2.php?actor_first=Stepin&actor_last=Fetchit

[58] www.wikipedia.org/wiki/Stepin_Fetchit

[59] http://www.ferris.edu/jimcrow/coon/

[60] http://en.wikipedia.org/wiki/Stepin_Fetchit

[61] Ibid, p. 1

[62] Ibid, p. 1

[63] www.dougmacaulay.com/kingspud/sel_by_actor_index_2.php?actor_first=Stepin&actor_last=Fetchit

[64] http://www.ferris.edu/jimcrow/coon/

[65] www.willrogers.org/wrbio.html

[66] www.willrogers.org/wrbio.html

[67] http://www.dougmacaulay.com/kingspud/sel_by_actor_index_2.php?actor_first=Stepin&actor_last=Fetchit

[68] http://www.black-cinema.org/blackcinema.html

[69] http://www.npr.org/templates/story/story.php?storyId=5245089

[70] Ibid, p. 1

[71] www.npr.org/templates/story/story.php?storyId=5245089

[72] http://en.wikipedia.org/wiki/Stepin_Fetchit

[73] http://www.black-cinema.org/blackcinema.html

[74] http://www.imdb.com/name/nm0275297/bio

[75] Ibid, p. 1

[76] http://www.ferris.edu/jimcrow/coon/

[77] Ibid p. 1

[78] Ibid p. 1

[79] http://en.wikipedia.org/wiki/Jack_Johnson_(boxer)

[80] http://www.bookrags.com/Jack_Johnson_(boxer)

[81] http://www.famoustexans.com/jackjohnson.htm

[82] Ibid

[83] http://www.bookrags.com/Jack_Johnson_(boxer)

[84] http://www.famoustexans.com/jackjohnson.htm

[85] http://www.si.umich.edu/CHICO/Harlem/text/jajohnson.html

[86] Ibid

[87] http://afroamhistory.about.com/od/jackjohnson/p/bio_johnson_j.htm

[88] http://en.wikipedia.org/wiki/Jack_Johnson_(boxer)

[89] http://www.famoustexans.com/jackjohnson.htm

[90] http://en.wikipedia.org/wiki/Jack_Johnson_(boxer)

[91] Ibid

[92] Ibid

[93] http://www.boxinginsider.net/columns/stories/92578430.php

[94] Ibid

[95] http://en.wikipedia.org/wiki/Jack_Johnson_(boxer)#_note-Burns

[96] Ibid

[97] http://www.boxinginsider.net/columns/stories/92578430.php

[98] http://www.famoustexans.com/jackjohnson.htm

[99] http://www.boxinginsider.net/columns/stories/92578430.php

[100] http://en.wikipedia.org/wiki/Jack_Johnson_(boxer)#_

[101] Ibid

[102] Ibid

[103] Ibid

[104] http://www.pbs.org/unforgivableblackness/about/

[105] http://en.wikipedia.org/wiki/Jack_Johnson_(boxer)#_

[106] http://www.pbs.org/unforgivableblackness/about/

[107] Ibid

[108] Ibid

[109] http://www.famoustexans.com/jackjohnson.htm

[110] http://en.wikipedia.org/wiki/Image:Johnson_jeff.jpg

[111] Ibid

[112] http://afroamhistory.about.com/od/jackjohnson/p/bio_johnson_
j.htm

[113] Ibid

[114] Ibid

[115] Ibid

[116] http://cyberboxingzone.com/boxing/jjohn.htm

[117] http://www.boxinginsider.net/columns/stories/92578430.php

[118] http://en.wikipedia.org/wiki/Jack_Johnson_(boxer)#_note-Burns

[119] Ibid

[120] Ibid

[121] http://www.famoustexans.com/jackjohnson.htm

[122] http://www.pbs.org/unforgivableblackness/about/

[123] http://en.wikipedia.org/wiki/Prohibition

[124] http://prohibition.osu.edu/content/why_prohibition.cfm

[125] Ibid

[126] Ibid

[127] Ibid

[128] http://en.wikipedia.org/wiki/Prohibition

[129] Ibid

[130] http://www.digitalhistory.uh.edu/database/article_display.
cfm?HHID=441

[131] Ibid

[132] http://en.wikipedia.org/wiki/Prohibition

[133] http://en.wikipedia.org/wiki/Prohibition_in_the_United_States

[134] http://en.wikipedia.org/ Prohibition_in_the_United_States#_

[135] http://en.wikipedia.org/wiki/

[136] http://en.wikipedia.org/wiki/Prohibition_in_the_United_States

[137] Ibid

[138] Ibid

[139] http://www.druglibrary.org/Schaffer/LIBRARY/studies/nc/nc2a. htm

[140] http://en.wikipedia.org/wiki/Prohibition_in_the_United_States

[141] http://en.wikipedia.org/ Prohibition_in_the_United_States#_wiki/ note-8

[142] Ibid

[143] http://www.geocities.com/Athens/troy/4399/

[144] Ibid

[145] http://en.wikipedia.org/ Prohibition_in_the_United_States#_

[146] Ibid

[147] http://www.cato.org/pub_display.php?pub_id=1017

[148] http://www.blackwell-synergy.com/doi/abs/10.1046/j.1468-5906.2003.00206.x?cookieSet=1&journalCode=jssr

[149] Ibid

[150] http://www.scgsgenealogy.com/rsch-Black.htm

[151] Ibid

[152] http://www.foursquare.org/landing_pages/8,3.html

[153] Ibid

[154] Metropolitan News Enterprise. (2007 August). http://www.metnews. com/articles/2007/mcpherson_at_mike.jpg.

[155] http://www.charismamag.com/display.php?id=12776

[156] Ibid

[157] http://www.assistnews.net/Stories/s06030162.htm

[158] Oral Roberts University. Holy Spirit Research Center. Azusa Street William Seymour. http://www.oru.edu/university/library/holyspirit/ seyaz.html

[159] West Angeles Church of God in Christ. Bishop Charles Harrison Mason. http://www.westa.org/azusa100d.html

[160] www.wikipedia.org/wiki/century of progress

[161] http://www.chicagohs.org/history/century.html

[162] Ibid

[163] http://century.lib.uchicago.edu/

[164] Ibid

[165] http://en.wikipedia.org/wiki/World's_Columbian_Exposition

[166] Ibid

[167] http://en.wikipedia.org/wiki/Century_of_Progress

[168] Ibid

[169] Ibid

[170] Ibid

[171] http://en.wikipedia.org/wiki/World's_Columbian_Exposition

[172] http://en.wikipedia.org/wiki/Century_of_Progress

[173] http://en.wikipedia.org/wiki/World's Columbian Exposition

[174] Ibid

[175] http://www.joancrawfordbest.com/biography.htm

[176] http://www.imdb.com/name/nm0186726/bio

[177] http://en.wikipedia.org/wiki/Joan_Crawford

[178] http://ctct.essortment.com/joancrawfordbi_rxhx.htm

[179] http://en.wikipedia.org/wiki/Joan_Crawford

[180] http://www.joancrawfordbest.com/biography.htm

[181] http://en.wikipedia.org/wiki/Joan_Crawford

[182] http://www.imdb.com/name/nm0001076/bio

[183] http://en.wikipedia.org/wiki/Joan_Crawford

[184] http://www.joancrawfordbest.com/biography.htm

[185] http://en.wikipedia.org/wiki/Joan_Crawford

[186] http://ctct.essortment.com/joancrawfordbi_rxhx.htm

[187] http://en.wikipedia.org/wiki/Joan_Crawford

[188] Ibid

[189] http://en.wikipedia.org/wiki/Joan_Crawford

[190] Ibid

[191] http://ctct.essortment.com/joancrawfordbi_rxhx.htm

[192] http://en.wikipedia.org/wiki/Joan_Crawford

[193] http://en.wikipedia.org/wiki/Joan_Crawford

[194] Ibid

[195] http://ctct.essortment.com/joancrawfordbi_rxhx.htm

[196] http://en.wikipedia.org/wiki/Joan_Crawford

[197] http://www.joancrawfordbest.com/biolast.htm

[198] Ibid

[199] http://www.imdb.com/name/nm0001076/bio

[200] Ibid

[201] http://www.imdb.com/name/nm0186726/bio

[202] http://ctct.essortment.com/joancrawfordbi_rxhx.htm

[203] http://www.imdb.com/name/nm0001479/

[204] Ibid

[205] http://www.clarkgable.com/

[206] http://www.clarkgable.com/

[207] http://www.imdb.com/name/nm0001479/

[208] Ibid

[209] Ibid

[210] http://www.imdb.com/name/nm0001479/

[211] Ibid

[212] Ibid

[213] Ibid

[214] http://www.clarkgable.com/

[215] http://www.imdb.com/name/nm0001479/

[216] Ibid

[217] http://en.wikipedia.org/wiki/Charlie_Chaplin

[218] http://en.wikipedia.org/wiki/Charlie_Chaplin

[219] Ibid

[220] Ibid

[221] http://www.amazon.co.uk/Charlie-Chaplin-Encyclopedia-Glenn-Mitchell/dp/0713479388

[222] http://www.tulsaworld.com/webextra/itemsofinterest/centennial/centennial_storypage.asp?ID=070321_1_CE9_spanc00037

[223] Ibid

[224] Ibid

[225] http://www.boeing.com/history/mdc/douglas.htm

226 http://www.boeing.com/history/mdc/douglas.htm

227 http://www.tulsaworld.com/webextra/itemsofinterest/centennial/centennial_storypage.asp?ID=070321_1_CE9_spanc00037

228 Gary D. Avey. Ford Model T Coupe.

229 The Old Car Manuel Project. http://www.tocmp.com/pix/N/images/Nash/18nash.gif

230 Photo Credit: Star Williams

231 Photo Credit: Star Williams

232 Photo Credit: Star Williams

233 Photo Credit: Star Williams

234 Photo Credit: Star Williams

235 Photo Credit: Star Williams

236 Photo Credit: Star Williams

237 Photo Credit: Star Williams

238 Photo Credit: Star Williams

239 Photo Credit: Star Williams

240 Photo Credit: Star Williams

241 Photo Credit: Star Williams

242 Photo Credit: Star Williams

243 Clem Boyd. "The Health Benefits of Prayer. www.family.org. Assessed on November 20, 2007.

244 Daniel Brown. Ezine Articles. Without Faith It Is Impossible to Please God.

245 Ibid

246 Ibid

247 Ibid

248 Ibid

249 Ibid

250 Daniel Brown. Ezine Articles. Without Faith, It Is Impossible to Please God.

251 Photo Credit: Star Williams

252 Photo Credit: Star Williams

253 Age Gauges. http://www.frontiernet.net/~cdm/age1.html

Dr. Gwen Williams

Dr. Gwen Williams is a Mother, Author, Evangelist, and Consultant. She is the mother of one daughter, Star Williams, who is Miss Oklahoma USA 2003 and made top ten in Miss USA 2003 pageant. Williams earned a Doctor of Ministry Degree in 1996, and a Master of Divinity in 1989, both from Oral Roberts University in Tulsa, Oklahoma. In 1984, she received a Bachelor of Science Degree in Accounting, specializing in For-Profit and Non-Profit Accounting. She did her undergraduate work at Indiana State University, Indiana Central College and Martin University.

Her professional experience is vast. She is the Chief Executive Officer of Life Enrichment Ministries for the past twenty years. Williams' work experience encompasses major positions pertaining to education, consulting, pastoring and leadership. Her administrative and leadership skills consist of overseeing the organization's missions, publishing, seminars, training, financial and budget development. Williams wrote numerous grants proposals, polity charts, business plans, evaluations, and organizational assessments. She held the title of "Field Education and Intern Program" supervisor where she trained 185 graduate and undergraduate students in the school of business, education, and theology.

She trained workers for twenty years in the Life Enrichment Missions Training program for overseas internships. Williams had the responsibility of educating up to 85 students who received missions certificates for cultural sensitivity, foreign relations, historical and practical training. Such as training nationals in music, home economics, nursing and hygiene, counseling, communication, drama, adult and youth ministry, and carpentry.

As a dynamic preacher & evangelist she pastored for four years in Seattle, Washington. She ordained, and trained pastors & ministers under Life Enrichment Ministries. In addition, she lived in England while studying the culture, writing curriculum, and researching for a faith-based ministry.

Gwen recently completed her second book entitled A New Wave of Refreshing: For the Nations Kingdom. Her first book is The Azusa Mission, which she co-authored with Bishop Otis G. Clark approximately 15 years ago.

Her mission is "Bringing Light and Life to Businesses, Homes, and Ministries, Coast to Coast and Around the World." As a missionary she has done just that when traveling to over 12 countries ministering and sharing the love of Jesus Christ.

Gwen is a faithful member at Victory Church in Oklahoma City, Oklahoma.

Official website: www.lifeenrichmentinc.com

Star Williams

Born in Indiana and raised in Oklahoma, Star Williams was brought up an only child by her single mother Gwen. Defying the statistics that said she'd be on drugs, pregnant out of wedlock, and delinquent Star was nurtured with the fear and admonition of God. To this day she has defeated those odds by remaining abstinent, not using drugs, and graduating with honors from Oral Roberts University, a Christian private school in Tulsa, Oklahoma. Star gives all glory and honor to Jesus Christ as she empowers other teens and young adults to live a vibrant, dynamic, and electrifying life of purity (1Tim. 4:12). Star believes that the message of holiness is not antiquated, just the medium in which it is being delivered. If the world could see virtuous lives being lived vivaciously and fully alive then maybe they would want to be participants too. She continues to inspire youth and adults alike that once you give your life to Jesus, he can and will keep you through a committed relationship with

Him. She passionately believes in the keeping power of the Holy Spirit (1 Cor. 1:8).

Star Williams is a full-time Minister of the Gospel of Jesus Christ as a Missionary

Evangelist. She has a passion for the unreached people groups of the world. She is also an author, mentor, life coach, and motivational speaker. Star was licensed as a minister in June 1999 by Life Enrichment Ministries, and Star was ordained April 2005 at Miracle Temple Church in Seattle, Washington under the direction of Bishop Otis G. Clark, Dr. Gwen Williams & Pastor Donald Jackson of Life Enrichment Ministries. Star stepped out on faith when she ended a lucrative career in corporate America to fulfill a dream and calling of "going into all the world and preaching the Good News to all creation." While in corporate America God blessed her sales, and Star as a twenty-two year old, one of the youngest representatives in her field, was able to meet tough quotas that put her in the top 7% of earners within the company nationwide and making over six figures a year. By putting God first Star is blessed to be able to travel all over the world preaching the Good News. She stands as a testament of what can happen when you let go and let God!

Star is also Miss Oklahoma USA 2003, and a Top 10 Semi-finalists in the Miss USA 2003 pageant. In addition to being Miss Oklahoma USA, she is also Miss Black Oklahoma 2001, and was 1st runner up to Miss Black International 2001.

Having a very high AQ (Adversity Quotient), Star is an enthusiastic runner and mountain climber. She completed a 26.2 mile marathon, and has plans to run the Boston Marathon. Through running she has learned more about what the body can endure through blistered feet, bruised toenails, and sore joints. Her favorite mountain to climb over 14,000 feet is Mount Belford in Colorado, which she climbed in 2004 to the peak. Amongst Star's many gifts include jewelry designer extraordinaire. Since 2007 Star has successfully run her own jewelry company (www.lovelyjewelry.net).

Additional accomplishments include being a radio Co-host of The Talk Show, and Vice-President of Life Enrichment Ministries, a missions & evangelistic organization. Her love of missions and the nations has taken her to over 12 countries including Holland, Japan, France, Costa Rica, Zimbabwe, Mexico, several countries in The West Indies, and England where she studied Broadcast Journalism and English Literature. Star received her Bachelor of Arts Degree with a major in Organizational & Interpersonal Communication from Oral Roberts University in 2003. She graduated Magna Cum Laude.

Over the years, Star has appeared on radio and television programs such as Miss USA live broadcast, Tulsa's Channel 2 KJRH's morning show, CNN's Talk Back Live, and twice on Make Your Day Count with Lindsay Roberts.

Her passion includes being a light and life to people by giving hope to the hopeless, love to the unlovely, and Christ to those who will receive him. Star lives her life based on Jeremiah 29:11, and strongly believes that God has GREAT plans for each and every person.

Star enjoys speaking to and motivating young people to persevere and live a victorious life to fulfill God's perfect will for their lives. She walks the walk that she talks, and continues to inspire and challenge youth worldwide to live a life in full abandonment to God. Star is faithfully planted at Victory Church in Oklahoma City, Oklahoma.

Official website: www.lifeenrichmentinc.com

Printed in the United States
105167LV00003B/139-168/P